UNDERSTANDING
ALTERNATIVE
MEDICINE

Jeanne Rattenbury

A Venture Book

Franklin Watts
A Division of Grolier Publishing
New York / London / Hong Kong / Sydney
Danbury, Connecticut

Photographs ©: Art Resource: 53 (The Board of Trustees of
the Victoria & Albert Museum); Corbis-Bettmann: 9, 19, 43,
63, 72; Dinodia Picture Agency: 59; Photo Researchers: 88
(Henny Allis/SPL), 6 (George Bernard/SPL), 84 (Paul
Biddle/SPL), 81 (Erika Craddock/SPL), 11 (LOC/Science
Source), 105 (Will & Deni McIntyre), 49 (Tim Malyon &
Paul Biddle/SPL), 68 (Hattie Young/SPL); Superstock, Inc.:
78 (Vallee des Reines-Tombe de Nefertari, Thebes/Giraudon,
Paris.), 24, 31, 35; Tony Stone Images: 90 (Yann Layma).

Illustrations by Janet Hamlin, and Vilma Ortiz-Dillon
Book design by Joan M. McEvoy

Visit Franklin Watts on the Internet at:
http://publishing.grolier.com

Library of Congress Cataloging-in-Publication Data

Rattenbury, Jeanne.
 Understanding alternative medicine / Jeanne
Rattenbury.
  p. cm. (A Venture Book)
 Includes bibliographical references and index.
 Summary: Introduces five alternative medical systems
and five major alternative treatments, including osteopathy,
traditional Chinese medicine, acupuncture, herbal medi-
cine, and massage therapy.
 ISBN 0-531-11413-9
 1. Alternative medicine—Juvenile literature. [1.
Alternative medicine.] I. Title.
R733.R385   1999
615—dc21   98-15669
                                              CIP
                                               AC

CONTENTS

INTRODUCTION

Many of us in the United States, Canada, and other modern Western countries have grown up thinking that there is only one kind of doctor. When we were sick, our parents took us to the pediatrician, a person whose name was usually followed by the initials "M.D." (for medical doctor). Most movies and television series about doctors reinforce the idea that medical practice is limited to M.D.s. As far as we were concerned, only a doctor could perform familiar tests and, based on the results, prescribe drugs or recommend surgery.

There are a couple of good reasons why M.D.s dominate the practice of medicine in the West. First, there are more of them than any other kind of doctor. Second, although their healing abilities may sometimes seem miraculous, we know that the medications they prescribe and the procedures they perform have been tested during scientific trials. If you are involved in a serious automobile accident or if you are born with a hole in your heart, nobody can give you a better chance of surviving than a licensed M.D.

The dawn of the twenty-first century, however, is finding more and more patients looking beyond their regular doctors for answers to their health questions. In the process, these patients are discovering alternatives to Western medicine that have been around for thousands of years. How did these other forms of medicine

4

become almost completely overshadowed by the *conventional medicine* practiced by M.D.s? And why is it that, despite its remarkable achievements, conventional medicine has lost the confidence of so many patients? A look at medical history—ancient and recent—will provide some answers.

Medicine in Ancient Times

In ancient times, medical art and science went hand in hand. "Science" referred to the explanations people use to understand disease, while "art" referred to their practical efforts to restore health. When primitive people first observed illness, they tried to explain it. Some said that sickness was a punishment from the gods. Others believed that illness occurred when an evil spirit gained control of a person's body. This was their science. In these societies, witch doctors or tribal medicine men were important figures. Their art involved using charms, spells, or religious rituals to drive the spirits away. This kind of medicine is still practiced in some parts of the world.

Next, early people theorized that illness was the result of imbalances among various forces or substances found within a person. In different cultures, these factors were interpreted somewhat differently. The ancient Chinese theorized about opposite forces called *yin* and *yang* and about five natural phases of matter known as fire, wood, earth, metal, and water. Ancient Indians thought about three forces, or *doshas*, called *Vata, Pitta*, and *Kapha*. In the fifth century B.C., the Greek physician Hippocrates developed the idea of the *four humors* (black bile, yellow bile, blood, and phlegm). All these ideas assumed that each force affected a person physically and emotionally. Ancient people didn't separate body, mind, and spirit. All three were considered part of the whole human being.

This photo shows a marble bust of the ancient greek physician Hippocrates. He proposed the theory of four bodily humors.

Based on these scientific *models*, the art of medicine centered around keeping these forces in balance. Using available materials and careful observation, ancient peoples started experimenting with the use of diet, exercise, fresh air, sunlight, sleep, *massage*, and herbs—the roots, bark, leaves, and seeds of plants—to heal. These techniques, along with lifestyle changes and other hands-on treatments, remained at the heart of health care for many centuries. In fact, this kind of health care has never been abandoned in China and India.

Western Medicine Charts a New Course
In the West, the art of medicine remained essentially unchanged for almost 2,000 years after Hippocrates' death. During this period, relatively few advances were made in

medical science. Following the fall of the Roman Empire in 476, Europe descended into a period when acquiring and defending territory was considered more important that studying and learning. In the eleventh century, the first universities and medical schools were established in Europe. These schools collected existing knowledge from the Greeks, Romans, and Arabs. But there was still little progress in medical science.

Starting in the fifteenth century, however, many changes occured in both the arts and the sciences. With more people living in cities and with the invention of the printing press, ideas and information were exchanged faster than ever before. To balance conflicting religious and scientific interests, people began to think of the body and spirit separately. As scientists learned more about individual body parts and systems, many doctors started concentrating on specific regions of the body and types of disease. In short, medicine became more specialized.

This specialization might be viewed as both the triumph of Western medicine and its major drawback. At first, however, specialization seemed to deliver nothing but benefits. Discoveries in chemistry resulted in powerful new drugs, including mercury, opium, and, much later, antibiotics. New knowledge of human *anatomy* and *physiology* helped doctors understand how the body functions. As a result, more diseases were identified and described, new surgical techniques were invented, and even more drugs were developed.

Alternatives Emerge in the West

At the same time that these advances were being made, patients were becoming increasingly dissatisfied with conventional medical care. While things were improving in the laboratory, in many ways they were becoming

7

worse in doctors' offices and hospitals. One factor was the natural time lag between basic science and applied science. That is, it can take decades for scientists to figure out how to make new findings useful to patients.

In addition, even when research did yield practical applications, many doctors never found out about them. Today the latest discoveries and techniques are reported regularly in monthly medical journals. And a great deal of this information is passed on to the general public via newspapers, radio, television, and on-line services. A couple of hundred years ago, on the other hand, news traveled much more slowly. As a result, some doctors prescribed powerful drugs without being aware of their toxic effects or performed surgery without first washing their hands. No wonder as recently as the late eighteenth century, Dr. Benjamin Rush—one of the United States' most famous physicians—still believed *bloodletting* (the removal of blood from people's veins) was a suitable medical *treatment* for just about any illness!

Against this historical backdrop, new forms of medicine began to challenge conventional medicine. As a rule, these challengers—*homeopathy, osteopathy, chiropractic,* and *naturopathy,* among others—rejected the idea that extreme measures were necessary to heal sick people. Interfering with natural processes often caused damage. Supporters of these new forms of medicine rejected conventional medical theory and treatments. They developed their own theories of health and disease. For instance, homeopathy was based on the idea that "like cures like," and chiropractic therapy was based on the idea that disease was caused by interference in the nervous system.

At the same time, some M.D.s also became increasingly aware that conventional treatments didn't always help—and sometimes hurt—their patients. These doc-

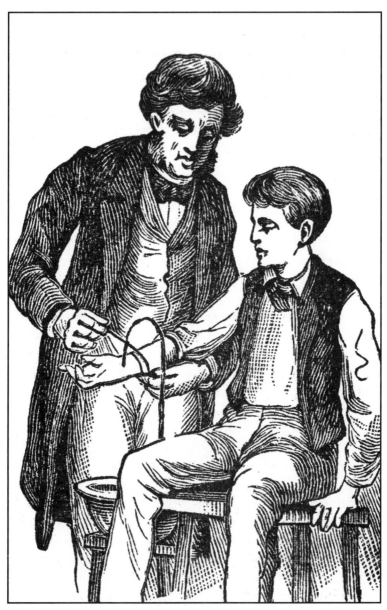

Bloodletting was one of the harsh medical treatments that led to gentler alternatives during the eighteenth and nineteenth centuries.

tors were in the minority, however, and their voices were rarely heard. Some of these dissatisfied M.D.s became skeptical of all medical theories. They decided to depend on results alone. If someone could prove through laboratory tests that a disease had a specific cause and clearly show that a particular treatment was effective, then—and only then—would they adopt that method.

Science Pays Off for Western Medicine

For a while, alternative doctors were actually more successful than orthodox M.D.s. This may be because their treatments didn't interfere with the body's own ability to fight disease, as harsh conventional medical treatments sometimes did. In the late 1800s and early 1900s, however, the tide turned back in favor of conventional medicine. This is because basic research began to provide answers to questions that doctors had been asking for centuries.

The work of three eighteenth-century scientists—Louis Pasteur, Joseph Lister, and Robert Koch—led to the idea that microorganisms, such as bacteria, cause all infections and some diseases. As this *germ theory* became accepted in the medical community, basic *public health* policies changed. (Public health involves protecting a community's health through sanitation, vaccinations, and other preventive measures.) People began to realize the danger of drinking water from the same rivers and lakes into which raw sewage was dumped. When the drinking supply was protected, the incidence of cholera and other infectious diseases declined sharply. Around the same time, the smallpox vaccine was developed. Because it was tremendously successful, scientists began to focus their attention on developing vaccines for other deadly diseases.

The French scientist Louis Pasteur (1822–1895) developed the "germ theory" of disease. Pasteur also developed pasteurization and a method of vaccinating patients against rabies.

The Flexner Report of 1910 also had a major impact on medical education. Backed by the Carnegie Foundation, a man named Abraham Flexner visited 155 medical schools across the United States to determine which ones were delivering the most scientific medical education. Flexner concluded that the *allopathic* medical schools (the ones that gave the M.D. degree) were doing the best job of educating physicians. Following this report, the government and private foundations stopped funding alternative medical education. By the early 1920s, more than one-third of the medical schools that had been in existence in 1900 had shut their doors. The majority of these were homeopathic, chiropractic, osteopathic, and naturopathic schools. Before long, these medical professions were virtually extinct. Around the same time, conventional Western medicine also began to dominate healing practices in Asia.

The twentieth century proved to be a golden age for Western medicine. Antibiotics were discovered in the 1930s, providing real cures for such formerly fatal diseases as tuberculosis and pneumonia. More vaccines were developed, including one for polio. New surgical techniques were refined. It is now possible to transplant organs or replace them with artificial ones. In addition, medical imaging technology has allowed physicians to see three-dimensional representations of the inside of the human body.

The Limitations of Conventional Medicine

Although alternative medical therapies started to fall out of favor in the late 1800s, today they are enjoying a comeback. The question is "Why?" The answer is that for all its strengths, conventional Western medicine also has weaknesses—some of which became apparent only because of its strengths.

While conventional medicine is excellent for treating *acute illnesses,* it is generally weak in treating *chronic* and *degenerative disease.* Acute illnesses have a rapid onset and a short, severe course. Examples include appendicitis and malaria. Chronic illnesses, on the other hand, generally last for a long time or recur frequently. Examples of chronic ailments include arthritis, asthma, migraine headaches, and back pain. Chronic ailments usually aren't fatal, but they can make life miserable. Degenerative diseases are characterized by a gradual deterioration—or wearing down—of tissues and organs. They include heart disease, cancer, and osteoporosis. In addition to being painful, degenerative diseases are often fatal. Ironically, because of Western medicine's success in treating acute illnesses, more and more people are living longer and are therefore more likely to suffer from chronic and degenerative ailments.

Western medicine does have tools—primarily drugs and surgery—for treating chronic and degenerative diseases. Unfortunately, these tools do not always eliminate the ailments and are often expensive. Patients diagnosed with high blood pressure in their thirties can spend tens of thousands of dollars on medication over a lifetime. The medicine won't cure the condition; it will just keep it in check. What's more, drug therapies often have unpleasant side effects, and surgery always holds the risk of complications.

Another common complaint about conventional medicine has to do with the relationship between practitioner and patient. Too many contemporary M.D.s treat their patients like machines to be fixed, rather than like human beings with feelings. Many doctors have become so dependent on diagnostic tests and high-tech equipment that they don't feel the need to listen to what their patients are saying. And even M.D.s with good "people skills" haven't necessarily learned how to help their patients maintain good health. Instead, some M.D.s know what to do only after their patients get sick. This has led some critics to label conventional medicine "disease care" rather than "health care."

Arguments For and Against Alternative Medicine

Alternative medicine is increasing in popularity because patients are dissatisfied with conventional medicine. Its main strengths are that it helps patients overcome—or at least live more comfortably with—chronic and degenerative conditions; it isn't very expensive; it rarely has harmful side effects; and it tries to make patients active partners in their health care.

Of course, alternative medicine has many critics. The number-one argument against alternative medicine is that it is unproved. In fact, "unproved" and "alternative" often mean the same thing to many critics. If an alternative treatment were sound, they reason, it would be brought into conventional medical care and would no longer be alternative. No matter how many individuals report that they have been helped by alternative medicine, such reports remain personal stories and therefore insignificant to the critics.

There are several responses to this argument. One has to do with economics. Medical research is normally funded by corporations that develop drugs or medical equipment and then sell it for a profit. Why would such companies spend millions of dollars to find out whether *acupuncture, herbal medicine,* or massage therapy works?

In 1992, the National Institutes of Health in the United States established an Office of Alternative Medicine to pay for studies that might confirm or dispute the claims of alternative treatments. Its budget is a fraction of what is typically spent on medical research.

In addition, supporters of alternative medicine point out that many alternative treatments do not lend themselves to double-blind studies—the only kind valued by conventional medicine. In a double-blind study, there are two groups of people—one is given a treatment, and the other receives something that seems like the treatment but is not (such as a sugar pill). Neither the participants nor the researchers are allowed to know who is receiving the real treatment. This is to guard against something called the *placebo effect,* whereby the patients' condition improves simply because they believe that they are being helped. By focusing on the whole person—mind, body, and spirit—

alternative medicine actively encourages the placebo effect, which makes double-blind studies useless.

Accusing alternative physicians of using unproved treatments is unfair in another sense. In 1978, a United States government report found that only 10 to 20 percent of the treatments commonly used by M.D.s had been tested by controlled studies. Drugs that are approved to treat one disease are often used to treat others, and new surgical techniques frequently become commonplace based on personal observation alone.

Another argument against alternative medicine is that it is dangerous. The danger doesn't lie so much in the treatments themselves, critics acknowledge. It lies in the possibility that serious conditions might go undiscovered and untreated if patients trust their health care to alternative practitioners rather than to conventional doctors. This is indeed a possibility, but it is actually a small one. Most people who seek alternative health care have already spent a lot of time and money on conventional care. They turn to alternative medicine only after conventional medicine has failed to help them.

A final argument against alternative medicine is that its practitioners are not qualified. Alternative medicine, however, is becoming increasingly professionalized, and its educational standards keep improving. In many locations, alternative systems and treatments are licensed by the government, which generally guarantees a high degree of skill. A license defines a profession's *scope of practice* (what license holders are legally allowed to do). It is not uncommon in the United States, however, for alternative practitioners to be licensed in one state and not in a nearby state. For example, two physicians might take an identical course in acupuncture but one may live in a state that offers a license in that field; while the second does not. Professions that aren't li-

censed often have their own rigid certification requirements. Not every alternative treatment sets such high
standards for its practitioners, but many do, so it is unfair to label all unconventional healers "unqualified."

The Future of Western Medicine

Happily, much of the distrust that has historically existed among health-care professionals with different
backgrounds is gradually melting away. Conventional
medical schools have begun to offer courses about alternative treatments. Hospitals are providing more
alternative options, especially in the area of *mind-body
medicine,* and some insurance companies are reimburs-
ing policy holders for treatments such as homeopathy
and *bodywork.*

In fact, the phrase "alternative medicine" is increasingly being replaced by "complementary medicine" as
it becomes more apparent that choosing a health-care
provider does not have to be an "either/or" proposi-
tion. Instead, patients and providers alike are realizing
that a team approach is often the best way to help people become and stay healthy. Many individuals have
important roles to play in the health-care process. If
you are interested in a career in health care, or if you
or a family member suffers from medical problems,
this book will introduce you to the world of alternative
medicine.

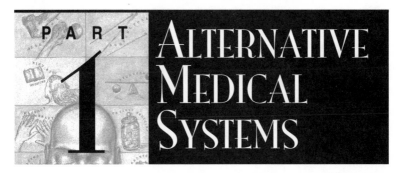

PART 1
ALTERNATIVE MEDICAL SYSTEMS

This section describes five alternative medical systems that train physicians to diagnose and treat patients. Osteopathy, chiropractic, and naturopathy were developed in the West in the past several hundred years. After enjoying brief success in the nineteenth century, they were overshadowed by conventional medicine in the twentieth century. Today they are being rediscovered.

Traditional Chinese Medicine and *Ayurvedic medicine* were developed in Asia approximately 5,000 years ago. They are not considered "alternative" in their countries of origin, where patients have access to both traditional and Western medicine. These ancient medical traditions are now gaining a foothold in the West for the first time.

Although each of these systems is different, they have several common features. First, they place great store in the self-healing ability of the human body. Second, they all recognize a natural force within each person that promotes and maintains life. Third, they take the whole person into consideration, rather than just one particular organ or disease. Individual doctors may choose to focus on specific disorders. But it is the official philosophy of each alternative medical system that mind, body, and spirit form a unified whole and that every part of the human body affects every other part.

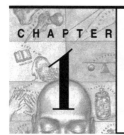

CHAPTER 1 OSTEOPATHY

Osteopathy is a system of medicine that focuses on the body's framework, or *musculoskeletal system.* This system, which consists of the bones and the muscles, supports the body and makes it move. Contemporary osteopathic physicians (D.O.s) have the same legal standing as medical doctors (M.D.s) in the United States and in a growing number of foreign countries.

History

Osteopathy was developed more than 100 years ago by Andrew Taylor Still, a Midwestern American physician. Still studied at the College of Physicians and Surgeons of Kansas City before enlisting in the Union army in the 1860s. He was trained in and practiced conventional medicine at a time when surgery was performed without anesthesia, and antibiotics and other effective modern drugs didn't exist.

To improve his medical practice, Still read everything he could find about medicine. He agreed with the ideas of Hippocrates, who believed that the human body was a unified whole. The body has the natural ability to heal itself, although it may sometimes need help. Still found that the musculoskeletal system had been neglected throughout medical history. But his observation of patients led him to conclude that this system plays a major role in the operation of other body parts.

Andrew Taylor Still (1828–1917) founded osteopathy.

When sore muscles made it difficult for a person to move, for instance, Still found that certain diseases got worse. Similarly, if musculoskeletal problems were corrected with hands-on treatments, other conditions often improved.

With these ideas as its foundation, Still developed a medical philosophy he called "osteopathy," a word that comes from the Greek words "osteon" (bone) and "pathos" (disease). By 1874, Still felt ready to share osteopathy with the medical world, but he was unable to find a forum for his ideas. Undiscouraged, he ultimately founded his own school with the help of his sons and several like-minded medical doctors. In 1892, Still started teaching classes in osteopathic medicine in Kirksville, Missouri. These classes were heavily grounded in anatomy and physiology. The first graduating class of the American School of Osteopathy was made up of seventeen men and five women—a male/female ratio that was extraordinary for the time.

Over the years, students of osteopathy increased in number. By 1896, there were 430 men and women studying in osteopathic schools in the United States. Vermont became the first state to pass a law licensing osteopathic physicians. In 1897, a group in Kirksville organized the American Association for the Advancement of Osteopathy (which later became the American Osteopathic Association). By 1906, the American School of Osteopathy had its own hospital complete with an x-ray machine—one of the first such machines west of the Mississippi River. By the time of Andrew Still's death in 1917, there were more than 5,000 licensed osteopaths in the United States, and the first school of osteopathy had been established in the United Kingdom.

Almost every state had laws permitting the practice of osteopathy by 1920. In 1957, the United States armed forces gave osteopaths military commissions. But American osteopaths were not granted the same scope of practice as M.D.s until 1973. At about that time, all fifty states legally recognized the training of osteopathic physicians as equal to that of M.D.s. Twenty years later, Osteopath's Bill of 1993 recognized British osteopaths as the first legal alternative health care practitioners in Europe. Despite these accomplishments, osteopaths are still not licensed as full physicians in Canada. In that country, they are limited to treating musculoskeletal conditions without drugs or surgery.

Today there are more than 38,000 licensed osteopaths in the United States, and the number is increasing steadily. Those who emphasize hands-on diagnosis and treatment do not mind it if other physicians consider them "alternative." Many others, however, prefer to use their medical licenses to practice conventional medicine as well.

Key Principles

Osteopathic medicine is based on the principle that up-keep of the musculoskeletal system is essential for good health. Bone and muscle make up approximately two-thirds of a human body's total mass, making the musculoskeletal system the body's largest system.

Because all body systems (musculoskeletal, nervous, cardiovascular, respiratory, and so on) are interconnected, osteopaths reason that keeping the largest of them healthy allows all of the other systems to work better, too. The musculoskeletal system not only has the most physical contact with the others (blood vessels and nerves pass through bones and muscle tissue, for instance), but it also requires the most energy. And a diseased musculoskeletal system uses more energy and resources than a healthy one.

Structure Affects Function

One way to understand osteopathic medicine is to compare the human body to a house. The house's floors, walls, and ceilings are like a body's bones and muscles. They make up its support structure. The water running through the pipes is like blood coursing through the veins and arteries in the cardiovascular system. Electricity moving through wires is like nerve impulses traveling through the nervous system. Heat flowing through duct work is like air passing through the respiratory system.

All of these systems are important parts of a house, and if any of them break down, the people living inside the house suffer. Usually each part doesn't break down completely, though. Instead, one pipe develops a leak. One wire develops a short. The house isn't perfect, but people can still live in it. It may be years before a leaking pipe causes the ceiling to collapse. If the walls start to sag, however, everything else begins to fall apart. The pipes, the wires, the ducts—all of these are inside the walls and cannot stay in good working order if the walls cave in around them. The water doesn't run. The power goes off. You can call a plumber or an electrician, but if you don't fix the walls, the problem won't go away.

Osteopaths try to keep the musculoskeletal system—the "walls" of the human house—from falling down. They do this by routinely observing and feeling the bones and the muscles in search of early signs of trouble. According to osteopathic theory, disease is preceded by a stage called *somatic dysfunction,* in which body tissues have stopped working properly. If this preliminary stage is detected, it can be reversed before disease sets in.

One result of this "structure affects function" model is that dysfunction somewhere in the musculoskeletal system may lead to disease elsewhere. Because the different body systems are interconnected, osteopaths sometimes find problems elsewhere in the body by paying close attention to the musculoskeletal system. People with kidney problems, for instance, often complain of pain in their back muscles. A diseased gallbladder can make a person's right shoulder hurt.

For prevention as well as treatment of disorders, osteopathic physicians literally provide "hands-on" help—massaging muscles and repositioning bones—although they often use other forms of treatment, too. Osteopaths do not believe that musculoskeletal imbalances are the only cause of disease. They do believe that the musculoskeletal system is involved in many disorders, however, and that treating bones and muscles will help a body return to good health.

Diagnosis and Treatment

A visit to an osteopath's office is similar to a visit to an M.D.'s office. After taking a patient's medical history, the D.O. asks about any current complaints. Depending on the nature of the complaint, the D.O. may order laboratory tests such as a blood test to look at blood chemistry or a magnetic resonance imaging (MRI) scan to look inside the body.

Many osteopaths, however, also employ a number of diagnostic methods that set them apart from the typical M.D. Osteopaths may check for any change from the normal spinal (or backbone) pattern. They may ask a patient to perform a series of movements, such as bending over and moving his or her arms in a circle. These tests help determine whether the patient's range of motion is limited in any way. They observe how a patient holds himself while standing, sitting, and walking, to see if any postural problems might help account for pain. They pay close attention to whether a patient uses one side of the body more than the other. And finally, they use their hands to feel, or *palpate*, the patient's body to check reflexes, muscle and skin tone, temperature, tenderness, and fluid retention.

An osteopath may determine that a patient's complaint has a biochemical cause, in which case the D.O. may prescribe medicines. The osteopath might determine that an internal organ is malfunctioning, in which case the D.O. might prescribe surgery. (Like M.D.s, some D.O.s are surgeons.) No matter what the source of the complaint is, osteopaths use a variety of hands-on techniques either alone or in combination with conven-

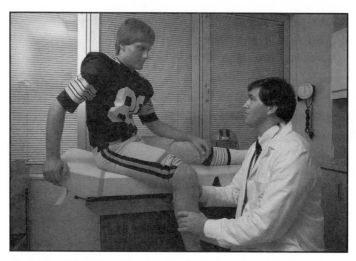

Osteopathic physicians use their hands to diagnose and treat injuries and other health problems.

tional treatments. Physical therapists have borrowed many of these osteopathic techniques.

When the movement of a patient's joints is limited, an osteopath may try to increase it by gently guiding a joint through its range of motion, slowly increasing the range over time. Or the osteopath may deliver a quick thrust to the joint. To ease muscle spasms, an osteopath may place the patient's body in specific positions that help reduce tension.

A treatment that is unique to osteopathic medicine is cranial manipulation, a gentle form of bodywork performed on the skull and the spine. Unlike massage, which typically involves the application of strong pressure, cranial manipulation is a slow, gentle attempt to influence the circulation of the fluid that surrounds the brain and spinal cord. It is used to treat headaches, jaw problems, and strokes, among other conditions. This treatment gave rise to a bodywork specialization known as *craniosacral therapy*. (See also pages 92–93 for a description of this method as a form of bodywork.)

Education and Credentials

To become an osteopathic physician, students must complete at least 8 years of schooling after high school. A bachelor's degree and significant course work in science (including biology, chemistry, and physics) are required for admission into accredited osteopathic medical schools. Interested students should also take the Medical College Admissions Test (MCAT) during their junior year of college.

After earning their D.O. degrees, osteopaths must complete residencies and internships at either osteopathic or allopathic hospitals before being eligible for their medical licenses. Licensed D.O.s may earn certification from the same medical specialty boards that certify M.D.s.

CHIROPRACTIC

Derived from the Greek words "kheir" (hand) and "praktikos" (effective), chiropractic is a system of promoting good health and treating disease primarily through hands-on adjustment (straightening or realignment) of the backbone and other joints. Spinal adjustments are performed because chiropractors believe that many diseases are caused by pressure on nerve pathways (the *spinal cord* runs through the center of the backbone). Early medical documents from China and Greece suggest that this technique was first used by these ancient cultures. Since its origin as a formal medical system in the nineteenth century, the profession has broadened its scope. Today many chiropractors work as primary-care physicians, treating a wide range of conditions with a variety of therapies, including nutrition counseling, in addition to spinal or *chiropractic adjustment.*

History

Chiropractic medicine was founded in 1895 by a self-taught American healer named Daniel David Palmer. One day Palmer met a janitor who had been deaf for 17 years following an injury to his upper spine. When Palmer delivered a thrust to the janitor's back, the janitor's hearing was restored. Although contemporary accounts vary, Palmer believed he cured the man by relieving pressure on a nerve involved in hearing. This is unlikely, however, as the nerve pathway from the ears doesn't even pass through the spine.

As a result of this incident, Palmer was inspired to develop the theory that all living creatures possess what he called an "innate intelligence," a force that flows through the central nervous system and controls body functions. Palmer theorized that disease occurs when this flow is disrupted by out-of-place *vertebrae* (the bones enclosing the spinal cord), which he called *subluxations.* According to Palmer, disease should be treated by straightening the spine. This would have the same effect as untangling a garden hose to let water move through it more freely. In 1897, Palmer opened the Palmer College of Chiropractic in Davenport, Iowa. Palmer's son B.J. was a natural promoter who used his Davenport radio station to mock conventional medicine and to promote his father's alternative system.

The earliest chiropractic education programs were brief sessions that focused almost exclusively on spinal adjustment. But by 1910, the National College of Chiropractic in Lombard, Illinois, had begun to offer courses in nutrition, *colonic irrigation,* massage therapy, and other forms of treatment. This set a precedent that other chiropractic schools followed. In 1913, Kansas became the first state to license chiropractors. The National Chiropractic Association (which became the American Chiropractic Association in 1964) and the Committee on Chiropractic Education were both formed in the 1930s. Thanks largely to the committee's recommendations, chiropractic education programs were expanded to four years. The education they provided allowed many graduates to pass the science examinations required to earn state medical licenses, though chiropractors were often refused licenses for political reasons.

In the 1960s, the bad blood that had always existed between chiropractors and M.D.s in the United States became the focus of a legal battle. At that time, the American Medical Association formed a Committee on Quackery and told its members that associating with the "cult" of chiropractic was unethical. In 1976, a group of chiropractors sued the AMA for violating antitrust laws by trying to monopolize medicine. More than a decade later, in 1987, a federal judge ruled in favor of the chiropractors, granting them the right to practice medicine without referrals from M.D.s. Today many hospitals have chiropractors on staff, and many chiropractors enjoy hospital admitting privileges.

There are currently more than 50,000 licensed chiropractors in the United States, treating more than 15 million patients each year. In addition, a growing number of foreign countries recognize chiropractic as a legitimate form of healing. These include Canada, South Africa, and Israel, among others.

Key Principles

As a profession, chiropractic practice is more divided than the other systems of alternative medicine described in this book. This is because some modern practitioners cling to the ideas upon which chiropractic was founded 100 years ago, while others support a form that takes into account the radical changes that have occurred in health care during the past century. What unites chiropractors is the belief that the human body has a self-healing ability and that hands-on adjustment of the spine encourages this healing process. What divides them is the degree to which they believe the spinal cord affects health and disease.

There is no question that the spinal cord is a key part of the central nervous system and that the ner-

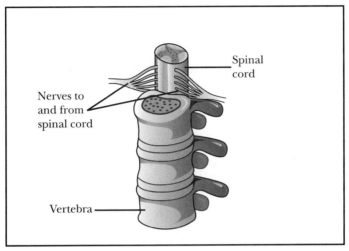

The spinal cord, a key part of the nervous system, runs directly through the center of the vertebral column. The purpose of chirocractic or spinal adjustment is to relieve pressure on nerves caused by misaligned vertebrae.

vous system controls many of the body's functions—digestion, circulation, respiration among others. The spinal cord is enclosed within twenty-four vertebrae. In the past, chiropractors theorized that subluxations—misaligned, but not necessarily dislocated, vertebrae—might put pressure on nerves. Some nerves must pass through the spine to reach major body organs such as the heart and the lungs. Therefore, early chiropractors theorized that pressure on those nerves could interfere with the function of those organs and lead to disease. Relieving the pressure on nerves through spinal adjustment, they reasoned, allows the organs to work more efficiently, improving health.

Most contemporary chiropractors think this theory has some validity but don't believe that spinal misalignment is the source of all illness. This is why chiropractic colleges offer courses in chemistry, anatomy, physiology, acupuncture, and clinical nutrition as well as courses in spinal adjustment. Still, most chiropractors maintain that regular chiropractic adjustment reduces wear and tear on the human body, in much the same way that having the wheels on a car aligned helps keep tires from getting worn down. Anyone who has walked with a limp because of a sore foot knows that compensating for pain in one part of the body often puts additional stress on another part of the body. Thus, chiropractic adjustment may help straighten out structural imbalances before they lead to other problems. Since the spine supports major muscle groups, chiropractors believe that spinal adjustment can relieve conditions associated with muscular tension.

Old-school chiropractors continue to think of the spinal cord as a sort of main switching station for the entire body. They maintain that spinal manipulation is appropriate treatment for many medical problems because it switches "on" the body's innate healing ability. Although many people—practitioners and patients alike—find this theory attractive, it is not supported by Western science. This doesn't necessarily mean that this theory is invalid—simply that it has not yet been proven.

Some chiropractors prefer to concentrate on relieving back and neck pain only, even if they are licensed as *primary-care physicians.* Others use the full range of their medical education to diagnose and treat all conditions that they can manage. They refer patients with more serious conditions to M.D.s, D.O.s, and specialists. Chiropractors who perform spinal adjustments only are known as "straights," while those who employ other techniques, such as acupuncture and nutrition counseling, are known as "mixers."

Diagnosis and Treatment

Chiropractors employ many of the diagnostic methods used by conventional physicians. They are trained to perform standard physical exams, which include taking detailed medical histories and ordering laboratory tests. In the United States, chiropractors are legally licensed to do so in more than half of the fifty states. If you have a sore throat, for example, chiropractors in many locales can order a throat culture to find out whether it is strep. They will not be able to prescribe antibiotics or other medication to treat that condition, however, and will often recommend that a patient go to an M.D. or a D.O. to get a prescription.

In addition to performing standard physical exams, chiropractors routinely consider other factors when making diagnoses. They measure the length of a patient's arms and legs and evaluate muscle tone. Using

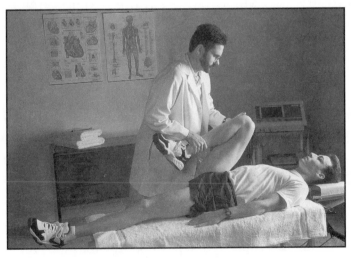

A chiropractor performing a physical examination

31

both their hands and high-tech instruments, they look for tension, stress, or abnormalities in bones and muscles. Chiropractors may also order x-rays of isolated parts of the body. These tests are used primarily to make sure the patient doesn't have a condition that shouldn't be treated with manipulation. These include fractures, which can be made worse by manipulation, and cancer, which can cause pain similar to that caused by musculoskeletal disorders. Subluxations are not visible on x-rays.

After determining a patient's physical status, chiropractors will treat the patient if they find a problem that can be helped by physical manipulation. In addition to back pain, conditions that respond well to manipulation include migraine headaches, infant colic, and carpal tunnel syndrome (a painful condition in which tendons of the wrist and the hand thicken and press on an adjacent nerve). If they identify a metabolic condition, such as high cholesterol or high blood pressure, chiropractors will usually treat the patient only if the condition is minor and can be controlled with diet and lifestyle changes. If a patient has a condition that requires medication or surgery, chiropractors commonly refer the patient to an M.D. or a D.O.

The main treatment tool used by chiropractors is known as the chiropractic adjustment. Chiropractors use this method to adjust joints throughout the body. Scientific research indicates that this technique is a safe and effective way to treat back pain.

Usually administered by hand, chiropractic adjustment consists of a very fast thrust to a joint to move it back into place. Although these thrusts often produce a popping sound (that's why chiropractors have been called "bone crackers"), they usually do not hurt. The popping sound comes from gas bubbles that are released from the fluid surrounding the joint. Patients usually lie on specially designed tables to receive such adjustments. Other techniques used by chiropractors to treat musculoskeletal disorders include massage, electrical stimulation, ice, heat, and, sometimes, acupuncture.

Education and Credentials

To become a chiropractor, students must complete at least 6 years of schooling after high school. Most chiropractic colleges require a minimum of 2 years of undergraduate education, including credits in biology and chemistry, and many require a bachelor's degree as a prerequisite for admission. To earn the doctor of chiropractic (D.C.) degree, candidates must complete 4 years of full-time study, covering many of the same subjects taught in allopathic medical schools, often using the same textbooks. Chiropractic colleges are accredited by the Council on Chiropractic Education, a group authorized by the United States government. As of 1997, there were eighteen accredited chiropractic schools in the United States, two in Australia, one in Canada, and one in England.

After earning their degrees, chiropractors must pass licensing exams before they can practice legally. Chiropractic *practice acts* (laws that define what a physician may do) vary from state to state. In some states, chiropractors are licensed as primary-care physicians. This means that they may diagnose, treat (without drugs or surgery), and/or refer patients for any health condition at their discretion. In other states, they may treat only musculoskeletal problems, just as dentists work only on teeth and optometrists work only on eyes.

CHAPTER 3

NATUROPATHY

Naturopathy is a long-standing system of medicine that became established under its current name about 100 years ago. Naturopathic medicine uses a variety of natural, nontoxic therapies to promote general good health and to combat minor illnesses. Such therapies include nutrition counseling, homeopathy, herbal medicine, bodywork, psychotherapy, acupuncture, exercise, and lifestyle modification. Naturopaths are trained as primary-care physicians, and in some locales they are licensed to prescribe mild drugs (such as antibiotics) and perform minor surgery (such as stitching up wounds).

History

Unlike chiropractic and osteopathy, which trace their origins to one strong-minded individual, naturopathy has roots in several different trends that arose in reaction to orthodox medical practice of the eighteenth and nineteenth centuries. These include *hydropathy* (now called hydrotherapy), the *Popular Health Movement*, and *eclecticism*.

Founded in Germany by a peasant, hydropathy was the practice of using water to promote good health. Hydropaths encouraged patients to drink large amounts of water and to apply it to their skin by taking baths, using hot and cold compresses, and so on.

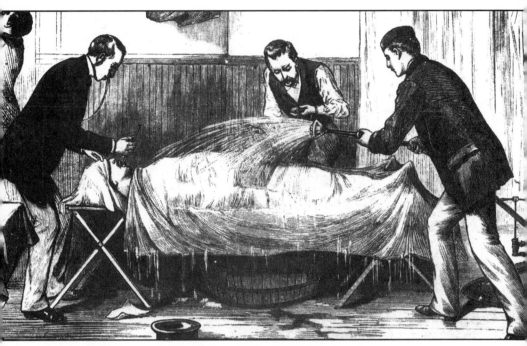

Hydropathy (now called hydrotherapy) uses water, both internally and externally, to promote good health.

A forerunner of the health-food craze of the 1970s, the Popular Health Movement was led by men whose names are household words today—Sylvester Graham (who invented the graham cracker) and J.H. Kellogg (who would no doubt disapprove of the sugar-coated breakfast cereals now sold by the company his brother began). Members of this movement were more than 100 years ahead of their time in questioning the healthfulness of caffeine, sweets, alcohol, eggs, milk, and meat.

Eclecticism was a nineteenth-century school of medicine. Its practitioners did not have a single philosophy. Instead, eclectics used whatever treatments—some conventional, some alternative—that they thought would work best. They might have given herbs to one patient and mercury to another.

Toward the end of the nineteenth century, a number of health-care providers began combining different natural therapies such as homeopathy, herbal medicine, special diets, and hands-on methods. These early practitioners of naturopathy were similar to eclectics, except they used only natural treatments. Contemporary naturopathy continues to be eclectic, borrowing from Asian medical traditions as well as from allopathic medicine.

The term "naturopathy" was coined in 1895 by John Scheel. By the early part of the twentieth century, naturopaths had started their own medical societies and opened their own medical schools. It wasn't long before most states began licensing naturopathic physicians. Like other unconventional systems of medicine, however, naturopathy fell into decline as allopathic medicine improved. Although all of the naturopathic medical schools eventually shut down, the doctor of naturopathy (N.D.) degree continued to be awarded by a handful of chiropractic colleges.

Thanks to a renewed interest in all things natural, naturopathy has made a comeback in the last few decades. There are now three 4-year postgraduate naturopathic medical schools in the United States. Each one is accredited by a government-approved council. These schools require many of the same courses that are taught in allopathic medical schools. In addition to such conventional subjects as anatomy, biochemistry, physiology, and *pathology*, naturopathic schools also offer instruction in homeopathy, acupuncture, herbal medicine, natural childbirth, and nutrition. Eleven states licensed naturopathic physicians as of 1994, and more than a million Americans use N.D.s as their primary-care providers. In addition, many other patients receive some of their medical care from naturopaths.

Key Principles

Naturopathy shares several principles with other alternative systems of medicine, starting with confidence in the healing power of nature. Naturopaths believe that the human body has a built-in ability to keep itself healthy but that this ability can be hampered by certain influences. These hindrances might relate to such personal factors as poor diet, a high-stress lifestyle, and heredity, or to environmental factors, such as dangerous chemicals. Naturopaths look for what is hindering the body's natural ability to heal itself and then work to remove that obstacle.

Naturopaths stress the importance of prevention, considering it their duty to teach patients how to minimize the risk of disease. Also, naturopaths take very seriously Hippocrates' instruction to "first, do no harm." This is why they prefer gentle, natural therapies. Naturopaths refer patients to M.D.s and D.O.s when an illness is too advanced to be treated naturally.

The Role of Symptoms

Conventional medicine tends to view *symptoms* as the unpleasant and unwanted result of disease. According to this way of thinking, a fever, for instance, occurs because an infection interferes with the body's ability to control its own heat. When patients' temperatures rise, M.D.s frequently advise them to bring their temperatures down by resting in a cool room, drinking cold liquids, and taking a fever-reducing drug such as acetaminophen. This may help reduce the fever, but it does nothing about the underlying infection.

Naturopaths, on the other had, tend to see a fever as a body's attempt to get rid of the microorganisms that caused the infection by making itself a less friendly place to visit. (Would you stay in a room that was too hot?) Under most circumstances, naturopaths will advise patients to let a mild fever (102°F [39°C] or less) run its course instead of interfering with the natural healing process.

As a rule, naturopaths are suspicious of medicines that make symptoms go away. To them, these drugs are like turning up a car radio so that you can't hear engine trouble. Moreover, naturopaths fear that a body can lose the ability to mend itself if its healing mechanisms are repeatedly turned off. The result is chronic illness, like the sinus infection that never seems to go away, and general deterioration of body tissues. Admittedly, symptoms are usually unpleasant, and most naturopaths recognize that suppressing symptoms is occasionally desirable for relieving a patient's suffering. But they don't make a habit of what they perceive as telling the body to "be quiet."

Disease as a Process

Most of us are probably used to thinking of disease as an enemy, as something that is battling against good health for control of a body. But that's not the way naturopaths see it. Instead, they see disease as the process a body goes through in an effort to stay healthy. It's like a war a country fights on its own soil. Though destructive, the war itself isn't the enemy. Instead, the enemy is any and all obstacles to good health. In fighting these, a body unfortunately must sometimes lay waste to its own territory.

In the early stages of a war, when outside forces are just beginning to invade, a good defense is often enough. Naturopathy is first and foremost defensive medicine. Its tools help a body become strong enough to withstand unhealthful influences. If a good defense isn't mounted early enough, however, the war may progress to the point where it's necessary to call in the backup troops—that is, the heroic medicine practiced by many M.D.s and D.O.s. Nowadays, naturopaths recognize that conventional medicine is sometimes necessary to treat advanced illnesses, and many N.D.s forge cooperative relationships with M.D.s.

Diagnosis and Treatment

To make diagnoses, naturopaths start by taking a detailed patient history, which includes questions about diet, lifestyle, and medications currently being taken. Naturopaths cannot prescribe most drugs, but they study pharmacology in school and are aware of the side effects of many medications. After performing a physical examination using familiar tools like stethoscopes, naturopaths often order and evaluate standard laboratory tests of blood, urine, and the like. When appropriate, they may also order throat cultures and x-rays.

Like primary-care M.D.s, naturopaths make certain decisions after their first examination of a patient. If they decide that the patient needs to see a specialist, they make a referral. If naturopaths are not sure of a diagnosis, they may order additional tests or consult with other physicians.

Naturopathic treatment is geared toward supporting a patient's own ability to stay healthy. Naturopaths may prescribe herbs or perform acupuncture to strengthen a body's organs and functions, or they may prescribe homeopathic remedies to stimulate healing. More than anything else, however, naturopaths focus on diet and nutrition. In fact, naturopaths receive ten times more training in clinical nutrition than do M.D.s. In addition to guiding patients toward healthier foods, naturopaths recommend dietary supplements when they think they are necessary. Naturopaths also try to identify foods that may be causing allergic reactions or otherwise interfering with a patient's health.

Naturopaths also provide treatments that improve blood circulation. This enhances health by bringing nutrients to various parts of the body and carrying away waste products (which end up in the colon, the bladder, and the sweat glands for excretion, or removal from the body). These treatments include physical manipulation (such as massage therapy) and hydrotherapy. Modern hydrotherapy involves the application of hot and cold water on the surface of the body to stimulate circulation.

Because naturopaths recognize symptoms as a body's effort to heal itself, they sometimes recommend treatments that actually intensify the symptoms, rather than suppressing them. For instance, since the body produces mucus to flush out irritants, instead of trying to dry up a runny nose, a naturopath may try to increase mucus flow by having the patient drink a mixture of lemon juice and red pepper.

In some states, naturopaths may prescribe mild drugs (such as antibiotics) and perform minor surgery (such as removing warts). A small number of naturopaths also use some more unusual treatments, such as *chelation therapy* and colonic irrigation. Chelation therapy is a method of removing minerals from a person's blood. When acid is injected into a patient's bloodstream, it binds with the minerals and guides them through the body for excretion. Although chelation therapy is an approved treatment for lead poisoning, its use for other purposes—such as clearing clogged arteries—remains controversial. Colonic irrigation removes fecal material from the colon (a section of the large intestine) by flushing it with water. (An enema cleans only the lower 12 inches [30 cm] of the colon.) Defenders of colonic irrigation claim that the buildup of feces in the colon can interfere with the absorption of nutrients and even lead to backaches. Skeptics contend that the procedure is anything but "natural."

Education and Credentials

There are many schools in the United States that grant the N.D. (naturopathic doctor) degree, but only three of them are accredited by the Council on Naturopathic Medical Education, a group approved by the United States government. These three schools are Bastyr University in Seattle, Washington; the National College of Naturopathic Medicine in Portland, Oregon; and the Southwest College of Naturopathic Medicine and Health Sciences in Scottsdale, Arizona. Students attending these schools are eligible for federal student loans. Only graduates of accredited colleges can be licensed as naturopaths.

To become a naturopathic physician, students must complete at least 8 years of school after high school—4 years of undergraduate education followed by 4 years of naturopathic medical school. The first 2 years of naturopathic medical school are dedicated to basic sciences, while the last 2 years focus on learning to diagnose and treat illnesses. After earning licenses, naturopaths may earn board certification in specialties such as homeopathy and acupuncture.

As of 1997, eleven out of fifty states licensed naturopaths. In some states, naturopaths are licensed as primary-care physicians, while in others their scope of practice is more limited.

CHAPTER 4

TRADITIONAL CHINESE MEDICINE

Traditional Chinese Medicine (also known as TCM) is an ancient health-care system that promotes balance and harmony of mind, body, and spirit. Its main tools are acupuncture, herbal preparations, and massage. TCM is used by one-quarter of the world's population. In China, it is used along with Western (allopathic) medicine. This chapter focuses on the history, key principles, diagnoses, and education under this medical system. Common treatment methods such as acupuncture and herbal medicine are discussed in detail in Part 2 of this book.

History

We do not know exactly when ancient Chinese physicians developed the complex principles on which Traditional Chinese Medicine is based. Fossils of needles made from bone, stone, and bamboo indicate that acupuncture was practiced as early as 5,000 years ago. By 200 B.C., all of the major concepts that characterize Chinese medicine as it is practiced today were described in a work known as *The Yellow Emperor's Classic of Internal Medicine.* This book is the first systematic compilation of medical knowledge written anywhere in the world.

For more than 2,000 years, the theoretical basis of Traditional Chinese Medicine has remained essentially

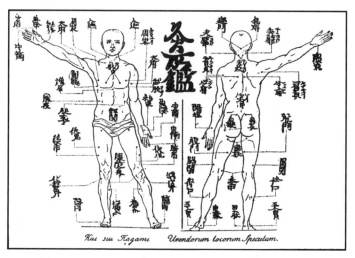

This chart from *The Yellow Emperor's Classic of Internal Medicine* identifies acupuncture pressure points on the human body.

unchanged, though its practice has been refined along the way. Previously unknown acupuncture points on the body have been identified, for instance, and the Chinese herbal *pharmacopoeia*—a list of medicinal herbs with information about their preparation and uses— has been expanded. In the eleventh century, during the Sung Dynasty, the first state-sponsored medical school was opened in China. This is about the same time that the first colleges of medicine were established in Europe.

Japan adopted Chinese medical techniques during the seventeenth century. Traditional Chinese Medicine remained pretty much unchallenged in the Far East until the nineteenth century, when powerful Western medical innovations, such as vaccinations and surgery, were introduced into Asia. Surgery had been performed in China more than 1,000 years earlier, but it had fallen out of practice. Convinced, however reluctantly, that Western medicine was superior, political leaders in China and Japan banned traditional medicine and withdrew government support for training in it.

China was never colonized by Europeans, and so its traditional medical practices were never outlawed by outsiders, as they were in India. Instead, a general desire to become more modern inspired democratic Chinese leaders to turn their backs on ancient traditions. When the Communist Party came to power in China in 1949, however, its leaders promoted TCM as a uniquely Chinese interpretation of medical science. Initially they did this because providing Western medical care to all Chinese citizens would have been prohibitively expensive. It soon became apparent, however, that the Chinese people supported their decision. They did not want to give up their traditional medical practices.

During the 1950s, the Communist government sponsored thousands of studies in an effort to quantify the effectiveness of Traditional Chinese Medicine. Researchers concluded that traditional medicine was worthy of financial support. This finding fit with Chairman Mao's political aims. Since that time, traditional medicine and Western medicine have been on an equal footing in China. Both kinds of medical education are available, and students and patients alike are free to choose whichever form they prefer.

Chinese medicine was introduced to Europe in the seventeenth century by returning Jesuit missionaries. It wasn't until U.S. President Richard Nixon's trip to China in 1972 spotlighted the use acupuncture for pain control, however, that Western countries really began to take notice. Since then, Chinese medicine has grown tremendously in popularity.

Key Principles

Chinese thought and Western thought are different in many ways, and this difference is reflected in Traditional Chinese Medicine. Western thought seeks to identify causes that help explain and predict phenomena. Chinese medicine is based on a different model of health and disease, and it uses poetic descriptive language to explain that model. There are clear links among Chinese philosophy, its agricultural past, and Chinese medicine. TCM sees the human body as a microcosm, or a reflection of the natural world, and describes it accordingly. The language of Chinese medicine uses words and makes comparisons that evoke images of the natural world. But this poetic language need not be taken literally in order to produce understanding of the nature of disease and effective treatment methods.

Qi

One of TCM's main beliefs is the existence of a vital life force called "qi" (pronounced chee). At one time, Western medical schools taught students about a similar life force; they stopped, however, because scientific instruments cannot measure this force. Qi is the energy that flows everywhere throughout the universe. The human body acquires qi from the environment. Once in the body, qi travels through pathways called *meridians* that run along the surface of the skin and inside the body. When qi circulates correctly through the body, harmony and balance result, and the individual enjoys good health. When qi is disturbed and doesn't flow smoothly, the result is disease.

Organs

Traditional Chinese Medicine does not view organs as material things, like the heart muscle or the liver gland.

Instead, it focuses on the activities performed by and interactions of groups of body parts. A lung, for instance, isn't just a spongy sac that occupies the chest cavity. It's the act of inhaling air through the mouth and nose, circulating it through the chest (where the oxygen in air is absorbed into the blood), and exhaling carbon dioxide. TCM recognizes twelve main "organs" (such as the liver, the heart, the gall bladder, and the spleen) and twelve lesser "organs" (such as the bone marrow and the blood vessels). Each organ is associated with physical, spiritual, and emotional properties.

Yin and Yang

Chinese descriptive metaphors derived from the classical work *Yijing (the Book of Change)* help describe the dynamic balance present in the universe as well as within human beings. Yin and yang are opposite forces

In ancient Chinese philosophy, yin and yang (represented above) are opposite forces that together form a whole.

that together form a whole. These forces must be kept in balance. In TCM, yin corresponds with the physical substance of an organ, while yang corresponds with its activity. An organ can be diagnosed as having either too much or too little yin or yang. In a similar way, many disorders in Western terminology have the prefixes "hyper" (excessive) and "hypo" (deficient). Yin corresponds not only to physical substance but also to qualities such as calmness, coolness, moistness, and stability. In addition to activity, yang is associated with agitation, heat, dryness, and changeability.

The Five Phases

Chinese medicine recognizes qualities in individuals that are similar to the properties of wood, fire, earth, metal, and water. (For example, wood is associated with growth and earth with stability.) These qualities are translated, rather inadequately, as "phases" or "elements." This complex system of phases is applied to all phenomena in the universe, including the organs of the body.

The relationship among the phases can be likened to the changing cycle of the seasons. Just as winter leads to spring, which leads to summer, then to fall, and to winter again, each Chinese phase gives rise to another phase and comes to dominate at a different point in the cycle. Individuals are believed to have all five phases represented within them in a dynamic state of balance. Imbalances among the phases result in symptoms and disease—both physical and emotional. Because of the dynamic relationship among the phases, an untreated imbalance in one phase ("too much wood," say, or "too little fire") leads to imbalances in all of the phases. The aim of the physician is to identify the primary imbalance and correct it.

Traditional Chinese Medicine holds that there are both external and internal factors that lead to the disharmony of body, mind, and spirit. External factors include heat, cold, dampness, wind, dryness, diet, and sex (usually too much rather than too little!). Internal factors include emotions such as anger, worry, sadness, fear, and even excessive joy, which is believed to strain the heart. The course of the disorder is shaped not only by these influences but also by the individual patient's constitution, which in turn affects the phase dynamics.

Diagnosis and Treatment

When TCM physicians examine patients, they do not look for the same things as Western doctors do. Above all, they are interested in the relationships among various symptoms. Chinese medicine maintains that certain types of imbalances produce one pattern of symptoms in one patient and a different pattern of symptoms in another patient. Because TCM physicians want to identify primary imbalances, a cough by itself doesn't mean anything. The physician has to consider other symptoms as well before a cough becomes significant.

Four main examinations help a TCM physician make a diagnosis. The first is a visual inspection. The physician looks at the patient's general appearance, taking note of his or her complexion (is it pale? ruddy?), build (slim? heavy?), and general temperament (relaxed? nervous?). The physician also inspects the patient's phlegm, vomit, urine, and other excretions. Most important, the physician examines the patient's tongue, paying attention to its color, texture, and moistness.

The second examination involves listening to the patient's voice (is it strong? weak?) and smelling body

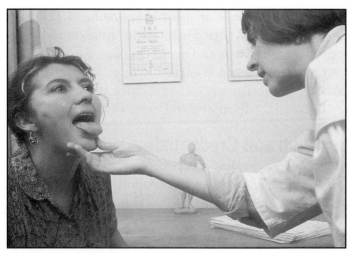
An acupuncturist examines a patient's tongue. Tongue inspection is an important diagnostic technique in Traditional Chinese Medicine. Different parts of the tongue are thought to mirror the state of various organ groups.

odors. Third, the physician asks a series of questions about the patient's medical history and about the complaint (usually pain) that brought the patient to the doctor in the first place. The physician asks about hot and cold sensations, headaches, dizziness, sleep habits, perspiration, thirst, and appetite.

Fourth and finally, the physician touches the patient's body at different points, primarily to determine the pulses in various parts of the body. Pulse taking in Traditional Chinese Medicine is much more elaborate—and is considered much more significant—than it is in conventional Western medicine. Chinese medicine recognizes twenty-eight different pulses that can be felt in three positions on both wrists. In addition to adjectives such as "slow" and "rapid," these twenty-eight pulses are described as being "soggy," "empty," "slippery," and "leathery," among other characteristics.

Together, these four examinations help TCM physicians determine the underlying imbalance that is producing symptoms. To correct an imbalance, the three main kinds of treatment that a practitioner of TCM will prescribe are acupuncture, herbal medicine, and bodywork (discussed in Part 2 of this book).

Education and Credentials

In the United States, there are about fifty schools of Chinese medicine that have been accredited by the National Commission for the Certification of Acupuncturists. Accredited programs take 3 to 4 years of full-time study to complete. Students entering American programs must have already earned at least 2 years of undergraduate credits including coursework in the basic sciences. Most students entering these programs have bachelor's degrees, and many of them have experience working in health care. Students may specialize in either acupuncture or herbal medicine. In China, it takes 5 years to complete TCM medical school.

In the West, doctors of Oriental Medicine (O.M.D.s) are generally not licensed as primary-care physicians, though they practice on an equal footing with M.D.s in China. As of 1998, thirty-eight states plus the District of Columbia licensed practitioners of Oriental Medicine, primarily to perform acupuncture. Legal scope of practice varies from state to state.

5 AYURVEDIC MEDICINE

Ayurvedic medicine, the oldest formal health-care system that is still practiced today, has much in common with Traditional Chinese Medicine. Ayurveda recognizes a life force, similar to the Chinese concept of qi, called *prana*. In the Ayurvedic tradition, the proper functioning of the body is linked with several forces called doshas. Ayurveda is also based on the idea that balance among the physical, emotional, and spiritual aspects of an individual is important for health. Imbalances are believed to weaken a person's resistance to viruses and bacteria. They also make a person more vulnerable to the stresses of overwork, inadequate sleep, poor eating habits, and personal crises. Ayurvedic physicians try to detect and treat imbalances before they lead to illness, though they also treat patients after disease has set in. Their main tools are nutrition counseling, massage, herbal preparations, and meditation.

History

Ayurveda is derived from the Sanskrit words "ayus" (life) and "veda" (science or knowledge). Its followers do not believe that Ayurveda was created or developed by human beings. Rather, it is thought to be the wisdom of the universe—a body of eternal knowledge that can be discovered by humans who have achieved a higher level of consciousness. According to tradition, the first sages "tapped into" Ayurveda in India up to 10,000 years ago. This learning was passed on orally for generations before the religious teachings known as the Vedas were put into writing around 5,000 years ago. Although Ayurveda includes instruction on how to maintain health and avoid disease, it is much more than just a system of medicine. Rather, it is a road map for achieving the highest and best state in every area of human endeavor—physical, intellectual, and spiritual.

The elements of Ayurveda began to be formalized around 3,000 years ago, during what is known as the Upanisadic Period of Indian history. The earliest surviving Indian medical texts were written about 2,400 years ago. Ayurvedic medicine was divided into eight branches (internal medicine; surgery; eye, ear, and throat; pediatrics; toxicology; psychiatry; rejuvenation; and sexual vitality) and two schools (the school of physicians and the school of surgeons). Ayurvedic physicians made some important scientific discoveries, such as the circulation of blood and the role of gastric juice in digestion, long before people in Western civilizations did.

Ayurvedic knowledge was passed from master to apprentice without serious interruption until the twelfth century A.D., when India was invaded by Muslims who favored Arabic medicine. Ayurveda regained government support in the sixteenth century under Mughal emperor Akbar the Great, who ordered that both Arabic and Ayurvedic medicine be compiled into a single book. Ayurveda suffered another setback in the nineteenth century, when India was colonized by Great Britain. The British Crown, which remained in power until 1947, actively discouraged many aspects of native Indian culture, including Ayurveda. Indian nationalists started reviving Ayurveda in the early 1900s, however.

**Ayurveda regained government support in India under Akbar
the Great, who ruled the Mughal Empire in the late 1500s.**

The first formal Ayurvedic medical college was opened in 1920. Today there are approximately 120 colleges of Ayurvedic medicine in India.

Ayurvedic medicine owes its growing popularity in the West to Maharishi Mahesh Yogi and Deepak Chopra, M.D. Best known as the founder of *Transcendental Meditation* (TM), the Maharishi adapted traditional Ayurvedic medicine into a less theoretical, more practical form called Maharishi Ayur-Ved. This system of medicine currently is practiced through special medical centers in about thirty countries. In addition to providing treatment for more than 100,000 patients since 1984, the centers offer training programs for licensed physicians. One of the thousands of M.D.s, D.O.s, and D.C.s who have become Maharishi Ayur-Ved "consultants" is Deepak Chopra, a Western-trained endocrinologist. Chopra has popularized Ayurveda through such best-selling books as *Quantum Healing, Perfect Health,* and *The Way of the Wizard.*

Although Ayurveda is regarded with a great deal of skepticism by the Western medical establishment, it is beginning to find support in research conducted at such respected institutions as Harvard and Stanford universities. In addition, the World Health Organization officially recognizes Ayurvedic medicine as an effective health-care system.

Key Principles

Central to Ayurvedic medicine is the idea that different factors create health and disease in people because people have different constitutions. In other words, people are simply different. Some people feel chilled at 60°F (16°C), while others feel warm. Some people need 9 hours of sleep, others get by with 7 hours. Stress produces headaches in some people and backaches in others.

According to Ayurveda, a person's constitution governs his or her mind, body, and spirit (in fact, Ayurveda does not separate the three) and is characterized by both strengths and weaknesses. A person's constitution is considered a blueprint for a variety of conditions—intolerance of certain foods, for instance, or a quickness to anger—that affect overall health. Each type benefits from a specific diet, exercise plan, and lifestyle. Similar symptoms may be diagnosed as having different causes when they are presented by individuals with different constitutions.

Vata, Pitta, and Kapha

Ayurvedic medicine recognizes ten mind-body types, or *pakritis,* which are controlled by the three forces called doshas. These doshas are Vata, Pitta, and Kapha. Vata (roughly translated as "motion") causes air to move from your nose to your lungs, food to move from your mouth to your stomach, and blood to move through your veins. Pitta (roughly translated as "metabolism") is the process by which the body transforms air and food into the energy necessary to sustain life. And Kapha (roughly translated as "structure") holds cells together to form bones, muscles, and fat.

In a descriptive rather than literal sense, the three doshas are thought of as being made up of the natural elements of space, air, fire, water, and earth, and are associated with certain qualities and seasons. Vata is composed of space and air. It is dry, cold, light, subtle, quick, moving, changeable, and rough. Its season is late autumn to early winter, when the air is dry and cold, and the wind is blowing things around. Pitta is composed of fire and water. It is moist, hot, light, sharp, fluid, sour-smelling, and slightly oily. Its season is midsummer through early autumn, when the air is dry, and heat makes things smell bad. Kapha is composed of earth and water. It is sticky, cold, heavy, sweet, slow, steady, soft, dull, smooth, and oily. Its season is spring and early summer, when the air is cool, heavy with rain, and filled with the sweet aroma of flowers.

Each of the three doshas is present in every individual, but to differing degrees. Generally speaking, a person who moves and talks quickly, is very emotional, and is on the slim side is said to have a Vata constitution. A person who moves and talks deliberately and forcefully, who is very regular and orderly, and who has a medium build is said to have a Pitta constitution. A person who moves and talks slowly, is calm and forgiving, and has a large build is said to have a Kapha constitution. Health results when all three doshas are in balance, but the balance differs from person to person. In many types, one dosha alone is dominant. In other body types, the person combines qualities from a second dosha as well. In rare instances, all three doshas may be represented fairly equally.

The doshas regulate a person's internal environment, but they are constantly reacting to external factors. A variety of influences—unresolved emotions, physical injury, the seasons, diet, lifestyle habits—are believed to throw the doshas out of balance. When this happens, ama (toxins) are produced. As ama circulates and builds up in the bloodstream, it interferes with prana (the life force) and immunity. The result is disease.

Most commonly, an individual's dominant dosha tends to exert more—not less—influence when it is out of balance. An out-of-balance Vata type often suffers from anxiety, irritable bowel syndrome, insomnia, and high blood pressure. An out-of-balance Pitta type (think hot and sharp) often suffers from anger, heartburn, and ulcers. An out-of-balance Kapha type (think moist and heavy) often suffers from depression, congested sinuses, and obesity. Left untreated, one out-of-balance dosha can drag the others out of balance. If this happens, a serious illness, such as cancer or heart disease, may occur.

Diagnosis and Treatment

According to Ayurveda, it is necessary to know a person's mind-body type before trying to diagnose and treat the patient. When an Ayurvedic physician, or *vaidya*, sees a new patient, the first thing he or she does is determine the patient's type through extensive questioning. These questions relate to physical concerns as well as interests, habits, and feelings. After determining that the patient is a Vata or a Pitta-Kapha, for instance, the vaidya asks additional questions about family history and the current complaint.

Although an Ayurvedic physical examination is quite different from the exams performed by Western doctors, there are some similarities. Like M.D.s, vaidyas listen to internal organs—but they do so without stethoscopes. Vaidyas analyze urine—but they do so without lab tests, relying instead on sight and smell. Like D.O.s, vaidyas use their hands to feel the patient's body and identify problems.

The most important diagnostic technique used in Ayurveda is a pulse reading. A skilled vaidya can distinguish between three types of pulses (Vata, Pitta, and Kapha) in twelve locations in the body. Pulse diagnosis is believed to provide much more information than just heart rate. It can supposedly detect dosha imbalances and their effects on specific organs. Vaidyas also pay close attention to the tongue, the eyes, and the nails, which are also believed to show dosha disturbances.

Once a diagnosis is made (such as aggravated Pitta), vaidyas prescribe a treatment program, which differs in details, depending on which doshas are disturbed. The first phase of treatment is getting rid of body impurities through a cleansing program known as *panchakarma,* which includes fasting, using enemas, and spraying liquid through the nasal passages. Even the blood is purified, by removing some blood (which is believed to stimulate production of new blood cells) and through the use of blood-thinning herbs.

The second phase is to bring the doshas back into balance through such techniques as eating a special diet, doing yoga (which includes breathing exercises), meditating, taking herbs, and lying in the sun for a short time. Diet is more important to Ayurvedic treatment than it is to other systems of medicine. This is because some foods are believed to aggravate the doshas, while others are believed to calm them. For instance, a person with a Pitta imbalance may be advised to eat apples but avoid apricots, or to eat chicken but avoid red meat and seafood. If following an Ayurvedic diet proves impractical, a person can sprinkle on his or her food special powders that are believed to affect the doshas.

The third phase of treatment is to strengthen the patient, through a different program of herbs, minerals, and exercise. As with diet, some kinds of exercise are recommended for certain mind-body types, while others are discouraged. The fourth and final phase is to improve mental and spiritual functioning by getting rid of emotional stress and negative thoughts. This is done through chanting, concentrating on geometric shapes, meditating, and using crystals. All these activities are believed to alter vibrations in the mind.

Yoga helps bring mind, body, and spirit back into balance.

Education and Credentials

The only country that offers full-time medical education in Ayurveda is India, where both Ayurvedic and allopathic medical schools grant the B.A.M.S. (Bachelor of Ayurvedic Medicine and Surgery) degree after 5 or 6 years of study. Unfortunately, it is almost impossible for foreigners to enroll in Indian medical schools because positions are reserved for natives.

In the United States, education in Ayurveda is offered through various institutions, but none of these programs is comprehensive. Perhaps the most substantial is Bastyr University's new specialization within its doctoral program, which leads to the degree N.D. (Ayurveda). Two British universities are in the process of setting up degree courses in Ayurvedic medicine.

Ayurveda is not recognized as a legitimate system of medicine in the West. No state in the United States licenses Ayurvedic physicians, so it is necessary for health-care professionals to have other valid medical licenses before they can practice Ayurveda legally.

PART 2

ALTERNATIVE THERAPIES

This section describes five major therapies that alternative practitioners use to help patients become well and stay well: homeopathy, acupuncture, herbal medicine, massage therapy and bodywork, and mind-body medicine. (The main therapies used in conventional medicine are drugs and surgery.)

In alternative medicine, therapies are not thought to "cure" ill health. Rather, they are intended to restore a body's ability to heal itself. It is not uncommon for more than one approach to be used at once. Alternative therapies may be prescribed or performed by physicians, but they may also be performed by laypersons, who have training other than full-time medical education.

6 HOMEOPATHY

Homeopathy is the practice of using small amounts of natural substances—which in larger doses would make a healthy person sick—to trigger the body's natural healing mechanisms. The name comes from the Greek words "homios" (like) and "pathos" (suffering). Homeopathy can be used to treat almost any type of complaint—physical or psychological—from burns and allergies to the effects of stress. Its basic philosophy, however, focuses on the prevention of illness. Homeopathic remedies are generally safe, nontoxic, and relatively inexpensive.

History

Homeopathy was developed in the late eighteenth century by a German doctor named Samuel Hahnemann. Hahnemann, like many pioneers in alternative medicine, was appalled by the harshness of conventional medicine. At that time, it was still common for doctors to cure disease by drawing dangerously large amounts of blood and giving patients strong chemicals to purge their systems violently. As a result, many sick people avoided doctors altogether.

Hahnemann wanted to find a gentler way of treating patients. In his reading, he had come across an age-old medical theory that "like cures like." That is, something that could cause a cough, for instance,

The German physician Samuel Hahnemann (1755–1843) founded homeopathy in the nineteenth century.

might also cure a cough. To test this theory, Hahnemann began experimenting on himself with quinine, a medicine that was known to be effective against malaria. After several days, he began to develop symptoms associated with malaria—chills, fever, and sweating. He continued working backward, testing other known medicines to see if they would cause symptoms similar to those they were used to treat.

Convinced that "the law of similars," as he called it, was valid, Hahnemann started experimenting with substances that had never been used as medicine before. If they caused a consistent pattern of symptoms in the majority of the people they were tested on, Hahnemann would then test the substances on sick people with those symptoms. If a substance helped cure the sick people, Hahnemann would add it to his list of proven homeopathic remedies. He eventually came up with approximately 100 of these proved remedies. Most of them derived from plants, but some came from minerals (such as sulfur) and even animals (such as snake venom). Today the homeopathic pharmacopoeia includes 2,000 remedies, which have been proved from tests of more than 4,000 substances.

To avoid giving his patients more medicine than they needed, Hahnemann conducted experiments to see how small the dose of medicine could get before it stopped helping patients. He diluted his medicines with water and alcohol. To his surprise, he found that the more dilute the dose, the more effectively the remedies worked. Homeopathic remedies are now made by diluting one part of the original medicinal substance (arsenic, say) with ten parts water or alcohol. After vigorous shaking, one part of the resulting solution is again diluted with ten parts water or alcohol. Sometimes this is done more than twenty-five times, producing solutions that cannot possibly contain even one molecule of the original medicine. Still, homeopaths maintain that these are the most powerful remedies of all. Hahnemann called this "the law of the infinitesimal dose."

Homeopathy was introduced in the United States in the early 1800s. It wasn't long before a number of conventional doctors started using homeopathic remedies. In Europe and North America alike, homeopathy was more successful than conventional medicine in treating many of that century's deadly diseases, such as cholera and scarlet fever. It is difficult to say whether this was because homeopathic remedies were truly effective or because harsh conventional treatments weakened patients. Homeopathic doctors soon started their own medical societies and opened hospitals and medical schools. Originally the medical schools of the University of Michigan and Boston University were homeopathic schools.

Homeopathy began to lose ground in the early twentieth century because of the great advances made in conventional medicine. Now that the limitations of conventional medicine are becoming more widely recognized, however, homeopathy is enjoying a revival in popularity. Although there are no longer any full-time homeopathic medical schools anywhere in the world, homeopathy is practiced by a wide variety of health-care providers. At last count, 40 percent of Dutch, 39 percent of French, 20 percent of German, and up to 37 percent of British physicians used homeopathy. It is also popular in Denmark, Sweden, Italy, Mexico, South America, and Russia.

The United States has been much slower to embrace homeopathy, but it is rapidly catching up. From the 1970s to the early 1980s, sales of homeopathic medicines grew by 1,000 percent in the United States. By the early 1990s, an estimated 2.5 million Americans were using homeopathic remedies. Homeopathy has been endorsed by the World Health Organization as a form of medicine that should be supported if the world is to achieve adequate health care by the twenty-first century.

How It Works

Science has yet to demonstrate exactly how homeopathy works. Its practitioners have theories that may or may not prove true. At the heart of homeopathic theory is the belief—shared by many systems of medicine—that the body has a natural ability to heal itself. Homeopaths believe the body's defense mechanisms are stimulated by the introduction of a foreign substance, in much the same way that vaccines activate the body's immune system against particular diseases or that allergy shots help the body learn to tolerate allergens.

Because homeopathic remedies are too highly diluted to operate on a chemical level, their supporters theorize that they may work on an energetic level. The energy of the medicine is believed to promote the individual's self-healing powers. The homeopathic remedy somehow retains the "memory" of the original substance, just as footprints may remain in the sand after a person has departed. Vigorous shaking of the remedy appears necessary to imprint this memory. These hypotheses have yet to be supported by laboratory studies, but future advances in quantum physics and technology may change that.

In the homeopathic model, illness is believed to reveal itself on different levels, from shallow to deep. Similarly, homeopathic remedies are believed to work on different levels, depending on their potency. Remember, the most highly diluted remedies are considered the most powerful. Outward physical symptoms, such as hives or headaches, are the least serious and can be treated with the least potent medicine. Internal symptoms, such as organ malfunction, are treated with middle-potency medicine. The deepest signs of illness lie in the spiritual or emotional state of a person. These are treated with the most potent (that is, the most highly diluted) remedies of all.

Although no one understands how homeopathic remedies work, a number of studies published in respected medical journals suggest that they are indeed effective. While critics of homeopathy insist that the remedies' success can be attributed to the placebo effect alone, scientific studies suggest that this is not necessarily true. For example, one study found that Nicaraguan children who were given homeopathic remedies recovered more quickly from extreme diarrhea (a leading cause of death among children in developing countries) than those children who were not. This study is particularly significant because it dealt with children, who are believed to be less susceptible to the placebo effect than adults.

Critics claim that not enough research has been done to support homeopathy. They also say that research supporting homeopathy is somehow faulty. Scientific studies cost a lot of money, however, and most of this money comes from pharmaceutical companies interested in medicines they can patent. Because homeopathic remedies are derived from natural substances, they cannot be patented. As a result, they generally do not attract research dollars. Supporters of homeopathy argue that it is unscientific to insist that a treatment cannot work simply because its mechanisms are poorly understood.

Types of Homeopathy

There are two main categories of practicing homeopaths: classical and nonclassical. Like Ayurvedic and TCM physicians, classical homeopaths believe every person has a unique constitution that must be identified before medication should be prescribed. A patient's outward symptoms are not enough to determine the appropriate remedy. Two patients can have similar symptoms but very different personalities and physical make-ups. Classical homeopaths spend a great deal of time (first appointments typically take about an hour and a half) getting to know their patients by asking a lot of questions. A patient often comes to a homeopath complaining about one or two symptoms.

A classical homeopath asks questions to determine a patient's constitution. Homeopathic medication, seen in background, is intended to cure illness by giving patients small doses of substances that produce the same symptoms.

But these question-and-answer sessions may reveal a variety of related symptoms. For instance, a person may be so accustomed to having difficulty sleeping that he or she doesn't consider it a health problem. Only after becoming familiar with both a patient's constitution and symptoms will a classical homeopath prescribe a remedy. This remedy should clear up all of the patient's symptoms by addressing their common underlying cause.

Nonclassical homeopaths, on the other hand, prescribe remedies based on patients' outward symptoms alone. All patients with sore throats, for instance, would be prescribed the same remedy. "Combination remedies" address symptoms that frequently occur together, as do the symptoms of the common cold. In the United States, homeopathic remedies are regulated by the Food and Drug Administration. The FDA requires that some homeopathic remedies be available by prescription only, while many others may be bought over-the-counter at drugstores. (Prescription remedies may be ordered by licensed medical providers only.) Homeopathic medicines come in several forms: tablets that are swallowed with water, pellets that are placed under the tongue, and liquid drops. Unlike some herbs, they are generally harmless if used incorrectly.

Education and Credentials

There are no full-time homeopathic medical schools anywhere in the world, but courses in homeopathy are taught at naturopathic medical schools and at special seminars. Homeopathy is not licensed in the United States, and there is no national certification exam. Most people who practice homeopathy—physicians, nurse practitioners, dentists, and veterinarians—have valid health-care licenses.

CHAPTER 7

ACUPUNCTURE

Developed more than 5,000 years ago in China, acupuncture is a technique for treating illness by stimulating tiny points on the surface of the body. Acupuncture is usually performed with hair-thin needles. But heat, finger pressure, suction, or electrical impulses are also used. Legend has it that acupuncture was discovered when a soldier recovered from a long-standing illness after being pierced by an arrow in battle. Whatever the origin, many years of observation and experimentation with needles (made first from bone and wood, and later from metals) led ancient Chinese doctors to conclude that certain points on the skin are associated with particular internal body functions and emotions.

Acupuncture was introduced to the West by Chinese immigrants in the nineteenth century. It wasn't until U.S. President Richard Nixon traveled to China in the early 1970s, however, that acupuncture began to receive widespread international attention. At that time, James Reston, a *New York Times* reporter who was covering Nixon's trip, fell ill while in China. After he underwent surgery for a burst appendix, the reporter's pain was treated with acupuncture. He was impressed with the results and wrote about his experience. His article ignited a firestorm of interest.

Today acupuncture is practiced by thousands of individuals in such countries as the United States, Britain, and Canada, not to mention many others in Asia. In the West, the majority of its practitioners have studied at North American and European schools of Eastern medicine. Acupuncture is also taught at naturopathic medical colleges as well as at some chiropractic colleges. In addition, an increasing number of M.D.s are learning acupuncture, often through special short courses. Traditionalists object that learning how to insert needles without accepting the principles of Traditional Chinese Medicine will not yield the best possible results. This is because, according to TCM, two people with similar symptoms may have very different disorders, depending on what kind of imbalance led to the symptoms. Different diagnoses call for the stimulation of different acupuncture points. This approach contradicts Western medical thinking, which generally supports prescribing the same treatment to different people with similar symptoms.

The World Health Organization cites 104 conditions as being appropriate for acupuncture treatment. Supporters of acupuncture believe that it can relieve just about any health disorder. Today acupuncture is frequently used in the West to treat addiction and mental disorders as well as physical ailments.

How It Works

Acupuncture is based on the theory that there are fourteen narrow pathways that direct energy flow among parts of the body, much as wires conduct electricity in a building. These pathways are called meridians. According to Traditional Chinese Medicine, energy (or qi) traveling through these meridians sometimes gets blocked or stuck, causing pain and illness. Through mechanisms that are only beginning to be understood in Western scientific terms, acupuncture

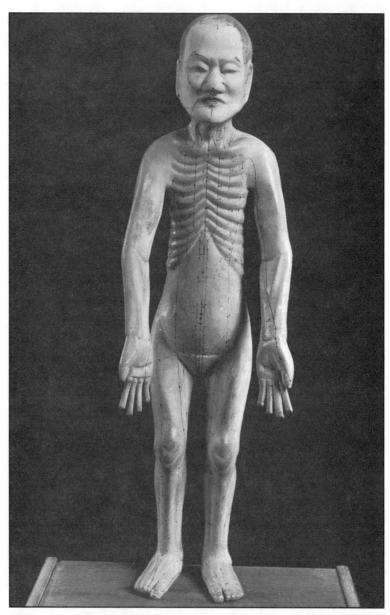

This porcelain model identifies meridians and acupuncture points. During acupuncture, needles are placed at specific points along the body.

seems to allow this energy to flow freely again, resulting in reduced pain and improved general health.

If you look at a diagram of the meridians on a Traditional Chinese acupuncture chart, you will probably be reminded of pictures of blood vessels or nerve fibers. In fact, though, the meridians do not correspond directly with any of the anatomical structures identified by Western medicine. Each meridian is associated with a particular body function, such as breathing or digestion. In addition, each meridian has points along its pathway that can be stimulated with acupuncture. The shortest meridian has nine acupuncture points, while the longest has sixty-seven.

Supporters of acupuncture believe that it enhances the flow of energy along a meridian in the same way that jiggling a television antenna can improve reception. This, in turn, strengthens the related body function. For instance, exciting acupuncture points on the liver meridian will help the body process toxins in food, alcohol, and drugs. Not surprisingly, many Western doctors are not willing to accept this explanation of how acupuncture works, even when they have observed its effectiveness. Other Western doctors dismiss acupuncture completely. They insist that acupuncture is scientifically unsound and that any benefits derived from its use are due to the placebo effect. The fact that acupuncture has been used successfully on small children and even animals, however, suggests that something other than the placebo effect is at work.

During the last quarter of the twentieth century, many studies have investigated the mechanism behind acupuncture. Although the results help explain acupuncture's effectiveness in some cases, such as in pain relief or as an anesthetic, other successful uses of acupuncture remain a mystery. Some scientists have found that many acupuncture points are near places where nerve endings meet muscle or bone. This suggests that the meridians share certain characteristics with neural pathways. It is important to stress, however, that the meridians do not correspond directly with the nervous system. Other scientists have found that acupuncture treatments may trigger the release of *endorphins,* which are natural painkilling chemicals found in the brain, the spinal cord, and the pituitary gland.

As for how acupuncture improves general health, recent research has unearthed relationships among

OTHER METHODS OF STIMULATING ACUPUNCTURE POINTS

- Acupressure is the application of pressure to acupuncture points with the fingertips. Sometimes considered a form of bodywork, acupressure really has more in common with acupuncture than with massage. Though not considered as powerful as traditional acupuncture, acupressure can be used when needles are not available. People can even do it to themselves. Acupressure can be used for averting asthma attacks, for example.

- Auriculotherapy is a form of acupuncture in which as many as 120 points on the outer ear are stimulated. The technique uses needles, massage, electrical impulses, or infrared rays. Developed by a French physician, auriculotherapy uses the ear as a mirror of the body. That is, points on the ear are believed to correspond with organs and functions elsewhere in the body. Some scientists theorize that the ear may act as the main acupuncture center because, in this area, the powerful vagus nerve is near the surface.

meridians, acupuncture points, and electrical currents running through the body. Someday, when the electromagnetic properties of the body are better understood, our questions about acupuncture may be answered definitively.

Types of Acupuncture

In general, acupuncture is performed with hair-thin stainless-steel needles that are inserted into (and sometimes through) the skin at acupuncture points. Most people do not find this painful, although they may feel a momentary pricking sensation or warmth.

- Cupping uses a glass cup (or other container) to stimulate acupuncture points. A small match is briefly placed under the cup. After the match is removed, the cup is applied to the skin over the acupuncture points. Because the flame consumes the oxygen in the cup, creating a vacuum, the cup sticks tightly to the skin.

- Moxibustion stimulates acupuncture points by igniting sticks or a cone of the dried moxa herb (also called mugwort, or *Artemisia vulgaris*). The herb is held close to the skin to produce a warming effect. Some practitioners believe that other herbs are equally suitable. When these herbs are used, this procedure is called heat treatment or cautery. Because the heat may cause pain and scarring, a piece of fresh ginger is sometimes placed between the flame and the skin.

- Shiatsu, or "finger massage," is a specific type of acupressure developed in Japan. Pressure is applied to acupuncture meridians and pressure points with the fingertips, the knuckles, the thumbs, the elbows, and the knees.

Education and Credentials

Individuals may learn how to perform acupuncture in various educational settings. Colleges of Eastern medicine offer the most extensive programs. In North America, about fifty programs are either accredited or in the process of becoming accredited. Students enrolled in naturopathic and some chiropractic medical schools may also take elective courses in acupuncture. In addition, special educational programs in acupuncture are available to licensed physicians.

To practice legally, acupuncturists have several options. Licensed physicians can generally perform acupuncture in the political regions (states, countries, and so on) where they hold valid medical licenses, even if they have never studied acupuncture. In the United States, the credential that carries the most weight is certification by the National Commission for the Certification of Acupuncturists, which generally assures that the acupuncturist has graduated from an accredited program. Although in some cases, the NCCA certificate may validate equivalent education. Of the approximately 7,000 acupuncturists in the United States, more than half have earned this certification. NCCA-certified acupuncturists can usually earn licenses in places that license acupuncturists. As of 1997, thirty-two states and the District of Columbia licensed acupuncturists.

8 HERBAL MEDICINE

More than 75 percent of the most commonly used prescription drugs are derived from plants. One example is digitalis, a medicine for heart disease that comes from the foxglove plant. Although many ancient healers dedicated their lives to discovering the hidden medicinal properties of plants, very few modern M.D.s have the knowledge to advise their patients that chamomile can calm an upset stomach, garlic can lower blood pressure, lobelia can ease sore throats and coughs, and witch hazel can reduce hemorrhoids. Yet, the use of plants and their parts for healing is the essence of herbal medicine, one of the most ancient forms of medical treatment. Herbal remedies have remained in continuous use in parts of the world where people have limited access to doctors. In fact, an estimated 84 percent of the world's population relies almost exclusively on herbal medicine.

History

Fossils from a 60,000-year-old Neanderthal grave site suggest that plants have been used to treat illness since prehistoric times. Early written records—first from China and India, and later from Persia, Egypt, and Rome—confirm that herbs were most likely humankind's first medicines. After the discovery of the Americas, friendly Native American tribes—who were

Herbal medicine has been practiced in many cultures for
thousands of years. This illustration represents Nefertari, an
Egyptian Queen (1314–1200 B.C.), using herbal medicine.

excellent herbalists—shared their knowledge with European settlers.

Some early herbal lore was built upon magic and symbolism. Sometimes a particular plant was used to treat a disease because the plant's shape or color resembled that of the diseased organ. For example, kidney beans were eaten to strengthen the kidneys. Similarly, snakeroot was used to treat a snakebite, wormroot was used to cure patients with worms, and bloodroot was used to prevent bleeding. More often, however, herbs were chosen for their healing properties—even though the reasons for their success were unknown. Interestingly, modern studies are showing that many animals instinctively know which plants to eat when they are sick.

Through the centuries, knowledge of the healing properties of herbal remedies was passed on orally from generation to generation. Medieval and Arabic herbals—early books about plants—contained huge compilations of drugs that could be derived from plants. Somewhere along the way, however, herbs fell out of favor with medical professionals in Europe and its colonies. When physicians began receiving more formal education, they began to feel it was beneath their talents to prescribe treatments that common peasants had mastered. Later this attitude was extended toward the treatments of Native Americans, whom colonists preferred to think of as ignorant savages.

During the Enlightenment, when the science of chemistry was developing, plants were considered unpredictable—varying in composition from specimen to specimen. How were doctors ever to come up with standard dosages? Furthermore, the lack of a uniform naming system for plants made plant identification somewhat difficult. Doctors decided to focus their attention on minerals such as mercury, which acted consistently (even though, ultimately, it was more toxic).

In the nineteenth century, chemists began isolating the medically active ingredients of herbs. The other parts of the plants seemed unnecessary. The early pharmaceutical industry didn't care for herbal medicine, any more than the medical establishment. Unlike synthetic drugs, plants could not be patented. Not only were herbal remedies effective but they were inexpensive, providing direct competition for the synthetics that drug companies produced.

While neglected by most conventional doctors in the United States, herbs are prescribed by physicians and sold in neighborhood drugstores in many Western European countries. In addition, herbal medicine is central to the practice of Ayurveda, Traditional Chinese Medicine, and naturopathy. There are also countless lay herbalists, who have not earned any medical degree. They must be careful not to make diagnoses, however. It is against the law to diagnose medical conditions without a valid medical license.

How It Works

Herbs must be compared with both food plants and manufactured drugs to explain how they work in the human body. In both instances, the action is chemical. Like fruits and vegetables, herbs contain vitamins, minerals, and other nutrients that help keep every cell in the body in good working order. When eaten, herbs enter the body's various systems the same way food plants do. They are broken down chemically in the stomach by special protein molecules called enzymes and absorbed into the bloodstream, which carries food molecules to distant cells and organs.

Aromatherapy uses the essential oils of herbs and flowers. They may be masssaged into the skin, inhaled, or added to bathing water. They may also be used to make creams, lotions, or perfumes.

Like manufactured drugs, medicinal herbs contain powerful components not found in everyday foods. These include alkaloids, essential oils, tannins, bitters, and mucilage. Alkaloids include morphine, caffeine, nicotine, quinine, and cocaine and are dangerous when taken in large doses. Essential oils give many herbs their distinctive aromas. Many act as natural antiseptics and antibiotics. Tannins help heal skin and other tissues. Bitters stimulate digestion. Mucilage soothes itching and swelling.

The difference between herbal medicines and manufactured drugs has to do with how they act upon living creatures. Herbs have smaller amounts of active ingredients, so their action is slower and less dramatic. When taken in their pure form, many modern medications have unpleasant side effects. They can even cause damage to the body when taken for extended periods of time. The National Center for Health Statistics reports that 125,000 people in the United States die each year from adverse reactions to prescription medicines.

There is evidence that the additional components of herbs—nutrients and the like—help balance the more powerful ingredients, thus eliminating the side effects that often occur when purified drugs are taken. For example, aspirin irritates many people's stomachs, but the herb meadowsweet, which works like aspirin, contains tannins and mucilage, which protect the stomach lining. Still, herbs are powerful enough that they should not be used carelessly. As a rule, bitter-tasting herbs are more potent than mild-tasting herbs.

METHOD OF ACTION OF HERBAL REMEDIES

The specific action of herbs can be broken down into a number of different categories:

- Adaptogenics support the adrenal glands, which help the body withstand stress.
- Alteratives help the body function properly.
- Anthelmintics (or antiparasiticals) expel or destroy intestinal worms.
- Antimicrobials help the immune system resist dangerous microorganisms. Antimicrobials include antibacterials, antivirals, and disinfectants.
- Antipyretics reduce or control fevers.
- Antispasmodics relieve muscle cramps.
- Astringents cause skin and other tissues to shrink, which reduces inflammation and irritation.
- Carminatives stimulate digestion and reduce gas.
- Demulcents reduce inflammation and irritation by drawing in moisture.

Most herbs have several actions. Chamomile aids in digestion, reduces inflammation, and helps people sleep. Peppermint counteracts nausea, diarrhea, headaches, and fevers. Because of their diverse characteristics, herbs can be used to treat a wide range of conditions.

Types of Herbal Medicine

Herbs are a mainstay of naturopathy, Ayurveda and Traditional Chinese Medicine, as well as less widespread forms of traditional medicine. Although different systems of medicine recognize the specific herbal actions described below, each system uses herbs in somewhat different ways.

Diaphoretics cause perspiration, which can relieve both fevers and chills.

Diuretics promote urination, which helps rid the body of toxins.

Emmenagogues regulate the female reproductive system, particularly menstruation.

Expectorants help clear mucus from the lungs and ease dry coughs.

Hepatics tone the liver, which helps remove toxins from the body.

Hypotensives reduce high blood pressure.

Laxatives promote bowel movements.

Nervines affect the nervous system, generally either revving it up or calming it down. Nervines include stimulants and sedatives.

Tonics revitalize organs and other tissues.

There are a variety of ways to use herbs therapeutically.

- Teas (also known as infusions and decoctions) are made by adding boiling water to herbs. Loose leaves and flowers can be allowed to rest in boiling water for 5 to 10 minutes (infusions), while tough roots and bark must be cooked continuously for about 15 minutes (decoctions) to release an herb's medicinal properties.

- Tinctures are very strong teas made with either alcohol or water.

A modern herbalist prepares a remedy. Herbalism is used widely throughout India, China, and other parts of Asia.

- Capsules and tablets resemble pharmaceutical drugs. They concentrate herbs, which sometimes taste unpleasant, into easy-to-swallow pills. The body absorbs these a bit more slowly than it does other herbal preparations.

- Poultices are made from bruised herbs, either fresh or dried, that are held together with a piece of gauze and then applied externally. They are often used to treat bee stings and cuts, among other conditions.

- Compresses are made by soaking a clean cotton cloth in an herbal tea for several minutes. They are then applied externally to areas of the body that are congested, inflamed, cold, or in pain. They can be kept warm with hot-water bottles.

- Essential oils are herbs in their most concentrated, distilled form. They must often be diluted with water or oil before being used because they are so strong. *Aromatherapy* is a branch of herbal medicine that works with essential oils and the sense of smell to produce various responses within a person's body.

- Salves are typically mixtures of essential oils and beeswax that are applied externally. Similar preparations include balms, liniments, and ointments.

Herbalists with a Western orientation tend to use herbs to treat certain symptoms or certain parts of the body. Fenugreek, for instance, is used to treat lung and sinus problems, fevers, and constipation. Lobelia is used to treat coughs, sore throats, and epilepsy. Rose hips are used to treat infections.

Ayurveda and Traditional Chinese Medicine, on the other hand, use herbs to alter the balance of a person's internal environment. In addition to the specific properties described above, herbs are thought of as cooling, warming, moistening, or drying. If a TCM practitioner diagnoses a patient as having "dry heat," for instance, he or she will prescribe herbs that are cooling and moistening. Similarly, if an Ayurvedic practitioner diagnoses a patient as having excess Kapha, which is characterized as cold and damp, he or she will prescribe herbs that are warming and drying.

Education and Credentials

Herbal medicine is taught in naturopathic medical schools and colleges of Eastern medicine, as well as in specialized herbology schools and programs. Because herbal medicine is not currently licensed anywhere in the United States, just about anyone can practice it. The National Commission for the Certification of Acupuncturists now administers a national certification examination in Traditional Chinese herbal medicine, but there is no national equivalent for clinical Western herbalism.

CHAPTER 9
MASSAGE THERAPY AND BODYWORK

Getting a professional massage might seem like a luxury, like going for a manicure or soaking in a whirlpool bath. Since ancient times, however, massage—the kneading, stroking, and movement of skin, muscles, tendons, and ligaments—has been used to promote healing all around the world. In Asia, documents indicate that massage has been an important health-care treatment for at least 3,000 years. In Europe, the famous Greek physician Hippocrates wrote 2,500 years ago that practical knowledge of massage therapy was an essential skill for doctors.

Like other traditional therapies, medical massage fell out of fashion in some parts of the West with the growth of powerful drug therapies and improved surgical techniques. Today, however, massage is making a dramatic comeback. In fact, massage therapy is the fastest-growing health-care profession in the United States today. Since its founding in 1943, the American Massage Therapy Association has seen its membership grow from 29 to more than 20,000. In many European and Asian countries, massage has never been abandoned by the medical establishment, and massage therapists are regularly employed in hospitals—a trend that is gaining ground in the United States.

Massage therapy is popular for several reasons. First and foremost, it feels good. In addition, unlike acupunc-

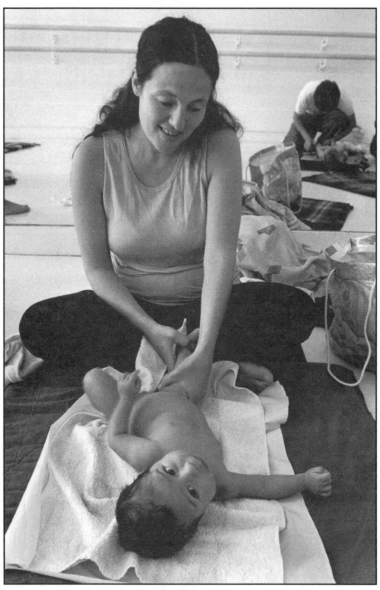

Massage involves rubbing and kneading areas of the body. Even small children may benefit from massage therapy. Daily massage has been shown to help premature infants gain weight more rapidly.

ture, homeopathy, and mind-body medicine, people don't generally view massage as a mysterious, new-age technique. Massage therapy is also relatively affordable. In enlightened countries such as Germany, it is even covered by national health insurance.

More important, massage therapy has been found to produce some remarkable results. Although adults often use massage therapy to manage pain—most commonly neck and back pain—it has a number of other applications as well. One study found that daily massage helped premature infants gain weight more quickly than those who were not massaged. The massaged babies were also able to go home from the hospital earlier. Another study found that people infected with HIV who received regular massages had more "natural killer cells" (cells that fight the AIDS virus and other threats, such as cancer) in their immune systems than patients who did not receive massage therapy. These cells were also more powerful than those of HIV-positive people who did not receive massages. Massage has even been shown to lower blood pressure, help wounds heal more quickly, reduce the swelling that often follows surgery, and relieve asthma and carpal tunnel syndrome.

Massage therapy is part of a larger field called bodywork, which includes a broad range of treatments. Some kinds of bodywork are distinguished by only the subtlest of differences, while others seem to have next to nothing in common with one another. What unifies them is that they are all based on relationships between two people, one acting upon the other in some physical way, without the use of chemicals (such as herbal or homeopathic remedies) and usually without tools (such as acupuncture needles). The physical nature of the relationship is what distinguishes bodywork from

Tai Chi is one type of bodywork. It combines meditation with a sequence of movements. This photo shows a group of elderly men and women practicing Tai Chi in Shanghai, China.

psychotherapy—another treatment based on interaction between individuals. Many proponents believe that bodywork can help people resolve emotional problems as well as physical problems.

How It Works

Massage therapy improves overall health by enhancing the circulation of blood and lymphatic fluid. As blood travels through the body, it brings nutrients to distant cells. As blood volume through a blood vessel goes up, the blood pressure goes down. That is good because high blood pressure is a risk factor for heart disease. The lymphatic fluid transports waste materials (such as dead bacteria) for elimination. In addition, many immune system cells travel in lymphatic fluid, which may explain why massage has been shown to improve immunity.

The pain-relieving effects of bodywork are undeniable. But its physiological mechanisms are still being unraveled. Muscles contract, or tighten, when they receive a message from the nervous system to do so. If this message is sent repeatedly—perhaps because of poor posture, heavy lifting, or emotional stress—the muscle may go into a painful spasm. Although scientists aren't sure exactly how, bodywork can interrupt the message to contract, which allows the muscle to relax. These therapies may interrupt the message through actual physical contact with the nervous system, or they may affect a person's mental state (after all, being touched is a basic human need). The mind may then send the message to relax.

Energetic bodywork is based on the idea that electromagnetic waves traveling through and around one person can be redirected by another person. We currently do not have the technology to test this belief. *Psychotherapeutic bodywork* starts with the idea that mind and body are interconnected and cannot be separated. Thus, a person may carry emotional trauma around in the form of muscle tension. Hands-on therapies are believed to be able to heal emotional scars by promoting the release of physical tension. Energetic and psychotherapeutic bodywork have not received much support from Western science.

Types of Bodywork

There are currently more than eighty kinds of bodywork, and new forms are being developed all of the time. Most practitioners divide bodywork into four major categories: message therapy, movement education, energetic bodywork, and Eastern movement therapy.

91

MASSAGE THERAPY

Many forms of body work are variations on massage therapy. That is, practitioners use their hands to manipulate the soft tissues of the body to reduce pain, correct physical imbalances, and promote relaxation. Some body workers focus on skin and muscle, others on tendons, ligaments, and facia— the connective tissue that encases a muscle like the thin skin around individual sections of an orange.

BODYWORK STYLE	ORIGIN OR THEORY
Swedish Massage	Developed by Per Henrik Ling, a Swede who visited China during the nineteenth century
Sports Massage	Physical therapy techniques
Reflexology	Has roots in ancient Egypt; modern system developed by Eunice Ingram and William Fitzgerald
Trigger Point Therapy (also known as myotherapy)	Developed by Dr. Janet Travell, based on ancient Chinese ideas
Craniosacral Therapy	Osteopathic technique invented by William Sutherland, a student of Andrew Still

ELEMENTS OF THE THERAPY	USES
Uses a system of long strokes, kneading, and friction techniques; chair massage is an abbreviated form limited to the neck, the shoulders, the back, the arms, and the scalp	Promotes general relaxation, improves circulation, and relieves muscle tension
Focuses mainly on the muscles relevant to athletic activities; shorter in duration and more vigorous than a full-body massage	Used before athletic activity to loosen muscles and afterward to help relieve pain, prevent stiffness, and return muscles to a normal state more rapidly
Applies pressure to points on the hands and the feet that are believed to correspond to other parts of the body	Corrects digestive problems, menstrual irregularity, fatigue, aches and pains, skin ailments, and chronic conditions affecting the elderly and children
Uses finger pressure on irritated areas in muscles to loosen knots and release spasms	Relieves chronic, recurrent pain of musculoskeletal origin
Applies light pressure to various points on the back of the head and the base of the spine to guide flow of cerebrospinal fluid	Augments self-healing powers; relieves headaches, painful sinuses, tinnitus, effects of menengitis, pain or strain caused by childbirth, and digestive disorders

MOVEMENT EDUCATION

Some forms of bodywork focus on teaching people how to move their bodies in ways that do not lead to pain or interfere with the proper functioning of various bodily systems. People who are habitually hunched over, for example, not only may suffer discomfort but often don't breathe efficiently either. Some movement-education bodyworkers have physical contact with their clients, while others don't touch their clients at all, acting more like teachers.

BODYWORK STYLE	ORIGIN OR THEORY
Alexander Technique	Western movement therapy developed by F. Matthias Alexander
Trager Approach	Method created by Chicago physician Milton Trager to help victims of polio
Hellerwork	Individual therapy based on the methods of Ida Rolf
Feldenkrais Method	Western movement therapy invented by Moshe Feldenkrais, an engineer

ELEMENTS OF THE THERAPY	USES
Helps individuals improve posture through hands-on guidance and verbal instructions	Combats fatigue; insomnia; stress and stress-related disorders; neck, back, and joint pain; and circulatory and digestive problems
Combines mental and physical exercises by client with gentle, rhythmic movements by practitioners to improve mobility	Relieves mobility problems, musculoskeletal disorders, asthma, headaches (including migraines), high blood pressure, and sciatica
Improves body alignment and flexibility through deep-tissue massage and movement education	Uses a preventive approach toward headaches, aches and musculoskeletal pains, and stress-related disorders
Helps improve coordination and flexibility through hands-on guidance and verbal instruction	Helps victims of stroke, spinal disorders, musculo-skeletal pain and injuries, chronic pain, and arthritis

ENERGETIC BODYWORK

A third broad category of bodywork is geared toward altering an individual's internal "energy." Practitioners include followers of Traditional Chinese Medicine, who try to direct the flow of qi along internal pathways, as well as physicians who don't follow Chinese models.

All practitioners of energetic bodywork maintain that energy flows through human beings and that it affects health and disease. Some believe that it is possible to have an impact on their clients' energy fields without even touching them. As a result, this kind of bodywork is often used on people who cannot be touched, perhaps because their skin has been burned. Hands-on energetic bodywork tends to be less vigorous than massage therapy.

BODYWORK STYLE	ORIGIN OR THEORY
Acupressure	Based on TCM energy meridians and pressure points to improve qi flow
Rolfing	Named for its founder, Ida Rolf, a biochemist who combined massage with bioenergetics
Polarity Therapy	Based on Ayurvedic principles; invented by Dr. Randolph Stone, naturopath, osteopath, and chiropractor
Therapeutic Touch	Energetic bodywork developed during the 1970s by nurse Dolores Krieger; variation of Japanese reiki

ELEMENTS OF THE THERAPY	USES
Uses finger-pressure massage; variations include shiatsu, jin shin do, and tuina	Soothes headaches, back pain, asthma, fatigue, and constipation; used in first aid
Uses very deep massage that softens fascia and returns the body to a state of balance	Alleviates musculoskeletal pain, poor posture, and breathing problems
Uses touch and diet, as well as physical and mental exercises and to balance the body's electromagnetic energy	Relieves allergies, headache, back pain, digestive and respiratory disorders, cardiovascular problems, and stress-related illnesses
Attempts to enhance natural self-healing abilities by holding the hands several inches away from patients' bodies	Eases physical, emotional, and spiritual conditions

EASTERN MOVEMENT

Eastern movement therapy is a collective term used to describe bodywork that focuses on balancing the flow of energy through the body with breathing exercises, basic movements, and body postures. Yoga can also be classified as a mind-body technique because it is part of a larger philosophy that focuses on achieving an inner state of enlightenment and uses meditation as well. But as a therapy, the body postures and movement exercises of yoga can help a variety of physical ailments.

BODYWORK STYLE	ORIGIN OR THEORY
Qigong	Chinese technique of movement and balance to direct the flow of life energies
Tai Chi	Popular oriental movement art based on energy flow of the body
Yoga	Based on the ancient Indian philosophical system

THERAPY

ELEMENTS OF THE THERAPY	USES
Uses relaxation, systematic movement, and visualization	Relieves chronic health problems, stress, sexual problems, and conditions caused by aging process
Combines basic sequence of movements with meditation	Reduces anxiety, muscular tension, blood pressure, and spinal and bone problems
Uses meditation, body postures, and breathing techniques	Aids recovery from injury; relieves stress, high blood pressure, asthma, digestive disorders, fatigue, and arthritis

Education and Credentials

Different kinds of bodywork have different training programs and certification standards. In the United States, the best overall guarantee of competency is certification from the National Certification Board in Therapeutic Massage and Bodywork. Most states that license bodyworkers use the same criteria as the board. Also significant is completion of a training program approved by the Commission on Massage Training Accreditation/Approval (an affiliate of the American Massage Therapy Association). This commission requires that students spend at least 500 hours in the classroom, including 100 hours of instruction in anatomy and physiology and 100 hours in such courses as first aid, CPR, and basic counseling.

CHAPTER 10 MIND-BODY MEDICINE

Everybody has heard the expression, "He [or she] died from a broken heart." It's usually used to describe people who, after losing someone very close to them—a mate or a child, for instance—lose the will to live and pass away. This may happen even if they had been quite healthy up until that time. People around the world have long recognized a connection between a person's psychological/emotional state and his or her physical health. This connection has given rise to certain stereotypes, such as the idea that aggressive, hostile people (otherwise known as "Type A personalities") are prone to heart attacks. It also accounts for the placebo effect. Today it is the basis for a group of techniques—known as mind-body medicine—that use mental exercises to treat physical ailments.

History

The ancient branch of medicine founded and practiced by Hippocrates recognized the interconnectedness of mind and body. This concept began changing in the West several hundred years ago. Though anxious to learn more about anatomy, medieval doctors had been forbidden to dissect human bodies because the Catholic Church (which controlled the legal and social structures of that time) maintained that Christians' bodies went to heaven after death. How could they enjoy eternal life if their bodies were cut up into pieces? To overcome this obstacle, the seventeenth-century French philosopher René Descartes argued that human souls were separate from their bodies. The soul remained the province of the Church, while the body became the province of medical science.

Freed from religious controls, Western doctors entered a period of extraordinary advances in medicine—one that continues to this day. Discoveries led to the creation of new medical models for understanding health and disease. The early study of anatomy generated the *mechanical model,* whereby the human body was viewed as a machine. Take the machine apart and you could figure out what was wrong with it and fix it surgically. Though incomplete, this model survived for several hundred years, until the discovery of germs by Louis Pasteur in the nineteenth century. At that time, the *biomedical model* began to take hold. This model viewed disease as being caused by outside agents (bacteria and the like) that could be neutralized with antiseptics, vaccines, and later, antibiotics.

Thanks to the mechanical and biomedical models, Western medicine is among the best the world has to offer when it comes to treating serious injuries and infectious diseases. However, these models have left certain questions unanswered: Why do some people stay healthy when exposed to the bacteria that make classmates or coworkers sick? Why do some people need heart surgery, while others don't?

Hans Selye, a researcher at McGill University in Montreal, shed some light on the subject with his discovery of the *fight-or-flight response* (also called the stress response) in the 1920s. In brief, the fight-or-flight response is a series of physiological changes that prepares all animals (including humans) either to run away from danger or to attack. When an animal feels threatened or scared, its heart beats faster, its breathing becomes shallow, more blood flows into its larger muscles, and its starts to perspire. Have you ever felt this way? Chances are, you have.

Recent research has revealed that while fight-or-flight can be extremely helpful in the short run, the long-term effect of this response is decreased immune function. Studies have also shown that humans don't have to be in real bodily danger to have this response—they just have to feel as if they're in danger. Stress isn't an event: it's how a person reacts to an event. Driving at high speeds delights some people, but it scares the living daylights out of others. Even something as simple as asking someone on a date is enough to trigger the fight-or-flight response in shy people.

It has become increasingly clear that while a disease may have only one cause (streptococcus bacteria alone cause strep throat, for instance), a variety of factors can make an individual vulnerable to a disease. Convinced that one of these factors involved how people handle stress—and life in general—an American doctor named George Engels proposed in the 1960s that the biomedical model be replaced with what he called the *biopsychosocial model.*

This new model of understanding health and disease didn't discard the important scientific discoveries of the past. Instead, it expanded upon them by taking into account information about patients' emotional and psychological states. Do they have a positive outlook, or do they tend to think that the deck is stacked against them? Did they recently go through a traumatic life event, like getting divorced or losing a job? Engel's idea went largely ignored for 20 years. During the 1980s, some fascinating breakthroughs occurred in a new interdisciplinary field called *psychoneuroim-munology (PNI)*. PNI explores the interactions among the nervous, immune, and *endocrine* (ductless glands that produce the chemicals called hormones) systems and how these systems are affected by emotions and behavior.

Most of the research in PNI can be divided into two broad categories. There are case studies in which psychological factors have been demonstrated to have a measurable effect on immunity. One study, for instance, found that medical students were more likely to become ill at exam time than at other times during the school year. Another showed that breast-cancer patients whose treatment program included support-group sessions and self-hypnosis lived twice as long as those who received conventional medical care alone.

Other studies document direct connections between the nervous, immune, and endocrine systems within laboratory settings. Using a powerful microscope, one researcher found nerve fibers in a patch of spleen tissue (the spleen is part of the immune system). Another found a stress hormone in a test tube filled with immune-system cells. Yet another researcher discovered that chemical messenger molecules previously believed to exist only in the brain are present throughout the entire body.

The details of PNI research are admittedly difficult to understand. What's significant is that PNI has made many skeptical scientists willing to accept that the mind does indeed influence the body. The result is that more and more hospitals are finding ways to add mind-body medicine to their treatment programs. Stress-reduction programs are common, and biofeedback equipment is becoming more widely available.

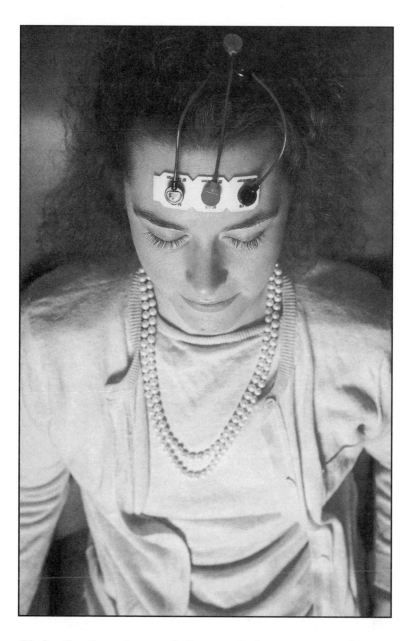

Biofeedback equipment helps people learn to control muscle tension and other bodily functions.

How It Works

Although scientific research has shown that different parts of the body communicate with one another, it is an overstatement to say that people can simply "will" themselves well. Still, there's a lot of evidence that positive thinking can make a difference, especially when combined with other forms of treatment. Mind-body medicine helps people improve their physical health through tech-

TYPES OF MIND-BODY MEDICINE

The following is a rundown of common mind-body techniques.

- Autogenic training is a relaxation technique in which individuals concentrate on certain parts of their bodies while thinking or reciting phrases such as "My body is sinking into the floor" or "I feel warm and peaceful."

- Behavioral medicine is a blanket term for techniques—such as biofeedback, hypnotherapy, and relaxation training—that prevent and treat disorders. Behavioral medicine is a recognized specialty within conventional medicine.

- Creative visualization is a technique in which a person concentrates on an image, such as a cancerous tumor shrinking or a skin rash clearing up. Guided imagery is based on similar principles.

- Biofeedback training uses sensitive electronic equipment to teach people how to control selected "involuntary" functions, such as body temperature and muscle tension. It is available primarily in hospitals and specialists' offices.

niques that redirect their thoughts away from fear, anxiety, depression, and other emotions that are believed to suppress the immune system while guiding them toward thoughts of joy, hope, and self-acceptance.

Many mind-body techniques try to undo the damage caused by the fight-or-flight response by focusing the attention away from sources of stress. In the late 1960s, an American doctor named Herbert Benson

- Breathing exercises use attention to the breath—usually deep, diaphragmatic breathing—to promote relaxation.

- Hypnotherapy uses the heightened suggestibility that accompanies the state of hypnosis to guide a person's thoughts in a healing direction.

- Meditation is any activity that keeps a person's attention grounded in the present moment. It typically involves sitting upright, adopting a passive attitude, and slowly repeating a mantra (a word or phrase such as "one" or "om") for at least 15 minutes.

- Progressive relaxation is the process of consciously controlling tension in voluntary muscles throughout the body, starting with the feet and moving through all the main muscle groups.

- Yoga promotes relaxation through a combination of breathing exercises, meditation, and physical postures.

did some research with several followers of Transcendental Meditation (TM) and found that these individuals could lower their blood pressure by meditating. In addition, meditation produced other physiological changes—including reductions in heart rate and respiratory rate—that were the direct opposite of the stress response. Benson named this the *relaxation response.* Since then, other mind-body techniques have been found to produce the relaxation response as well. These include autogenic training, yoga, progressive relaxation, and hypnotherapy. Touch therapies such as massage also bring on the relaxation response.

Other mind-body techniques combat stress by teaching people how to change their reactions to situations. Simply learning to be aware that you're responding stressfully to something is a good start. If you're getting uptight because bad traffic is making you late for an appointment, it's helpful to sit back and realize what's going on. It's also important to learn the difference between the situations you can control and those you cannot. If you discover that situations you can control are making you stressful, then you can change the situations. If driving on high-speed expressways makes you tense, for example, maybe the solution is to drive on side streets instead. If you can't control the situation, then you need to try to change your attitude. If you absolutely must drive on expressways, perhaps you should do it over and over again until you're comfortable with it. This is called *systematic desensitization.* These kinds of mind-body technique is often practiced in groups, with other people who are trying to make similar changes in their lives. The technique can also be practiced one-on-one with a therapist.

Yet another type of mind-body technique involves actively imagining that your physical illness is going away. Examples include guided imagery and creative visualization. Someone with cancer might envision cancer-fighting cells removing a tumor like pulling weeds from a garden, for instance, or someone with heart disease might imagine his or her clogged arteries opening up. This kind of mind-body medicine is regarded with more skepticism than stress-reversing techniques. The main argument in favor of it is that if it makes patients feel more powerful, their immune systems may well work better.

Like every medical treatment, mind-body medicine doesn't work for everyone, but if nothing else, it usually improves quality of life for patients who practice it. They may not be able to hold off death, but they are often able to face death peacefully and contentedly.

Education and Credentials

Mind-body medicine is such a diverse field that there are no educational standards that apply across-the-board to practitioners. Most practitioners are professionals who are already working in health care. They may be physicians, nurses, psychologists, or social workers.

In addition to whatever training they have undergone to prepare for their chosen professions, these individuals typically have taken special courses and attended seminars in mind-body medicine and its techniques. Although there is no general certification for mind-body medicine, certain subspecialties do have certification requirements. These include biofeedback and hypnotherapy. Because mind-body medicine is not licensed, some *laypersons* practice it as well.

AFTERWORD

The American philosopher, physiologist, psychologist, and teacher William James (1842–1910) once said that a new idea goes through three stages before it is accepted by the establishment. First, the idea is considered ridiculous, and the people who support it are called quacks. Second, the idea is found to be true but is dismissed as insignificant. And third, the establishment realizes the idea is both true and very important—and then takes credit for discovering it.

In the Western world, alternative medicine is now in James' second stage and is slowly creeping toward the third stage. Every year, more and more studies suggest that alternative medicine really does work. And while some members of the medical establishment may not place much stock in these studies, health-care consumers are buying into alternative medicine like never before. It is these consumers—not the studies—who are making conventional doctors stand up and take notice.

In this information age, patients are no longer dependent on their physicians for information about new medical treatments. Today magazines sold at every grocery store checkout counter contain articles about health issues. They often include information about alternative medicine. Acupuncture and homeopathy—topics that were once discussed only in obscure new-age journals—have now found a place in mainstream publications such as *Good Housekeeping, Life,* and *The Wall Street Journal.* Every library and bookstore in the United States carries a variety of books, such as the one you are reading right now, about alternative medical treatments. And the World Wide Web is fast becoming an extensive storehouse of conventional and alternative medical information. As people investigate alternative medical techniques and are impressed by their success, they will spread the word to friends and family members.

Conventional medicine is responding by incorporating alternative treatments into hospital programs and adding electives on alternative medicine to medical-school curricula. It is not difficult to foresee the day when insurance companies reimburse patients as readily for massage therapy as they do for back surgery. Will the medical establishment ever claim to have invented alternative medicine? Only time will tell whether the cynical William James proves to be right.

GLOSSARY

acupuncture—the stimulation of various points on the surface of the body to treat illness and promote general good health.

acute illness—a condition that has a rapid onset and a short, severe course, such as appendicitis.

allopathic medicine—the form of medicine practiced by medical doctors (M.D.s). Derived from the Greek word for "other," allopathic medicine often focuses on treating the symptoms rather than the root causes of illnesses.

alternative medicine—variety of medical therapies (some very new but others ancient) that rely on the body's natural healing ability and treat human beings as a complex blend of body, mind, and spirit. These therapies often complement rather than replace conventional medicine.

anatomy—the study of the shape and structure of organisms and their parts.

aromatherapy—a branch of herbal medicine that works with essential oils and the sense of smell to produce various responses within a person's body.

Ayurveda or *Ayurvedic medicine*—a traditional form of medicine that originated in ancient India, based on the idea that disease is caused primarily by imbalances within individuals.

biomedical model—medical model that sees disease as being caused by outside agents such as bacteria.

biopsychosocial model—medical model that expanded understanding of health and disease to include the effects of emotions and stress on the body's physical state.

bloodletting—the removal of blood from a person's veins to treat illness.

bodywork—a blanket term for a wide range of physical therapies including massage, movement reeducation, and treatments intended to alter internal energy.

chelation therapy—a method of removing minerals from a person's blood by injecting into the bloodstream an acid that binds with the minerals so that they can be removed.

chiropractic—a form of medicine that promotes health primarily through physical manipulation of the spinal column and the joints of the musculoskeletal system.

chiropractic or *spinal adjustment*—a very fast thrust to a joint to move it back into place.

chronic illness—a condition that lasts for a long time, or that recurs frequently during a person's life, such as asthma.

colonic irrigation—a method of flushing waste material and impacted feces from the colon (a section of the large intestine) with water.

conventional medicine—see *allopathic medicine.*

craniosacral therapy—the application of extremely light pressure to various points on the body to guide the flow of the fluid that surrounds the brain and the spinal cord.

degenerative disease—a condition characterized by a gradual deterioration of tissues and organs, such as heart disease.

dosha—one of three forces (Vata, Pitta, and Kapha) that practitioners of Ayurvedic medicine believe influence a person's mind, body, and spirit and are associated with certain qualities and seasons.

eclecticism—a nineteenth-century school of medicine whose practitioners did not cling to any one philosophy but used whatever treatments worked best.

endocrine—the system of ductless glands that produce chemicals called hormones.

endorphins—natural pain killing chemicals found in the brain and the nervous system.

energetic bodywork—a form of physical therapy that is geared toward changing the body's internal "energy."

fight-or-flight response—a series of physiological changes that prepare animals (including humans) to run away from danger or to confront it. Also called the stress response.

four humors—the four bodily fluids (blood, phlegm, yellow bile, and black bile) that in ancient Western medicine were thought to determine a person's general health.

germ theory—the idea that infectious diseases are caused by microorganisms. See also *biomedical model.*

herbal medicine—the use of the parts of plants (bark, roots, leaves, flowers, and so on) to treat illness and promote general good health.

homeopathy—the use of small amounts of natural substances to treat illness.

hydropathy—health reform movement that focused on the healing power of water.

Kapha—one of the three basic elements of Ayurvedic medicine, roughly translated as "structure;" it holds cells, bones, muscles, and fat together.

laypersons—practitioners who are not licensed professionals.

massage—the stroking and kneading of skin, muscles, tendons, and ligaments.

mechanical model—medical model that sees the body as a machine.

meridians—in Traditional Chinese Medicine, the fourteen pathways running along the surface of the skin and within a body that conduct the life energy, or qi.

mind-body medicine—a group of techniques that use

mental exercises to treat physical illness.

model—simplified representation of a phenomenon and the theories used to explain it.

musculoskeletal system—the body system, consisting of the bones and muscles, that supports the body and helps it move.

naturopathy—a system of medicine that uses a variety of natural therapies to treat illness and promote good health.

osteopathy—a system of medicine that places particular emphasis on the musculoskeletal system and uses hands-on methods to diagnose and treat illness.

pakritis—distinct mind-body types or constitutions according to Ayurvedic medicine.

palpate—to use hands to feel or explore an area of the body.

panchakarma—in Ayurvedic medicine, the elimination of impurities by fasting, vomiting, enemas, spraying liquid in the nasal passages, and using blood-thinning herbs.

pathology—the study of the origin, nature, and course of diseases.

pharmacopoeia—an official list of drugs, herbs, or other medicinal substances with information on their preparation and use.

physiology—the study of the functions of the cells, tissues, and organs of an organism.

Pitta—one of the three basic elements of Ayurvedic medicine, roughly translated as "metabolism;" it controls digestion and other biochemical processes.

placebo effect—the beneficial effect in a patient following treatment that comes from the patient's expectations about the treatment rather than from the treatment itself.

Popular Health Movement—reform movement of the nineteenth century that questioned the healthfulness of consuming too much caffeine, sweets, alcohol, eggs, milk, and meat.

practice acts—laws that define what a physician may legally do.

prana—in Ayurvedic medicine, the life force.

primary-care physician—a practitioner who is qualified to diagnose and treat common health disorders.

psychoneuroimmunology (PNI)—an interdisciplinary medical field that explores the interactions among the nervous, endocrine, and immune systems and how they are affected by emotions and behavior.

psychotherapeutic bodywork—type of bodywork that starts with the idea that mind and body are linked and uses hands-on therapies to promote the release of physical tension.

public health—the science and practice of protecting a community's health through sanitation, vaccinations, and other preventive measures.

relaxation response—a series of physiological changes that are the opposite of the fight-or-flight response.

qi—according to Traditional Chinese Medicine, the vital principle or life force.

scope of practice—what medical license holders are legally allowed to do.

spinal cord—the bundle of nerves that runs down the center of the backbone, controls the muscles, and carries sensory messages.

somatic dysfunction—according to osteopathic theory, the stage in which body tissues stop working properly, preceding the onset of disease.

subluxation—in chiropractic medicine, the partial dislocation of a bone in a joint.

symptom—a noticeable disturbance in normal body function.

systematic desensitization—a mind-body technique in which subjects progressively expose themselves to a stressful situation until they are comfortable with it.

Transcendental Meditation—a form of meditation developed by Maharishi Mahesh Yogi that promotes relaxation through repetition of a word or phrase known as a mantra.

treatment—measures taken to counteract illness. Legally, only licensed practitioners can prescribe treatments.

vaidya—a doctor of Ayurvedic medicine.

Vata—one of three basic elements of Ayurvedic medicine, roughly translated as "motion;" it controls circulation of blood, respiration, and the motion of food.

vertebrae—the individual bones of the backbone through which the spinal cord runs.

yin and *yang*—according to Chinese philosophy, the two opposite forces in the universe.

FOR MORE INFORMATION

Books

Beinfield, H. and E. Korngold. *Between Heaven and Earth: A Guide to Chinese Medicine.* New York: Ballantine Books, 1991.

Benson, Herbert. *The Relaxation Response.* New York: Avon Books, 1976.

Castro, Miranda. *The Complete Homeopathy Handbook.* New York: St. Martin's Press, 1990.

Chopra, Deepak, M.D. *Perfect Health: The Complete Mind/Body Guide.* New York: Harmony Books, 1991.

Complan-Griffiths, Michael. *Dynamic Chiropractic Today: The Complete and Authoritative Guide to the Major Therapy.* San Francisco: HarperCollins, 1991.

Coulter, Harris L. *Divided Legacy, a History of the Schism in Medical Thought, Vol. 3.* Washington, DC: Wehawken Book Company, 1973.

Cummings, Stephen and Dana Ullman. *Everybody's Guide to Homeopathic Medicine.* Los Angeles: Jeremy P. Tarcher, Inc., 1991.

Downing, George. *The Massage Book.* New York: Random House, 1972.

Foster, Steven. *Herbal Renaissance: Growing, Using, and Understanding Herbs in the Modern World.* Salt Lake City: Gibbs Smith, 1984.

Katpchuk, Ted. *The Web That Has No Weaver.* New York: Congdon and Weed, 1983.

Lad, Vasant, M.D. *Ayurveda: The Science of Self-Healing.* Wilmot, WI: Lotus Light Press, 1984.

Martin, Raquel. *Today's Health Alternative.* Tehachapi, CA: America West Publishers, 1992.

McIntyre, Anne. *Herbal Medicine.* Boston: Charles E. Tuttle Co., 1993.

Moyers, Bill. *Healing and the Mind.* New York: Doubleday, 1993.

Northop, George. *Osteopathic Medicine: An American Reformation.* Chicago: American Osteopathic Association, 1987.

Stellerman, Elaine. *The Encyclopedia of Bodywork.* New York: Facts on File, 1996.

Svoboda, Robert. *Ayurveda: Life, Health, and Longevity.* London: Penguin, 1992.

Trowbridge, Carol. *Andrew Taylor Still, 1828-1917.* Kirksville, MO: Thomas Jefferson University Press, 1991.

Vithoulkas, George. *The Science of Homeopathy.* New York: Grove Press, 1980.

Weiss, Rudolf Fritz. *Herbal Medicine.* Beaconsfield, England: Beaconsfield Publishers, 1988.

Organizations

American Association of Acupuncture and Oriental Medicine
433 Front Street
Catasauqua, PA 18032
610-433-2448
www.aaom.org

American Association of Naturopathic Physicians
601 Valley Street, Suite 105
Seattle, WA 98109
206-298-0126
www.naturopathic.org

American Botanical Council
P.O. Box 144345
Austin, TX 78714
512-331-8868
www.herbalgram.org

American Chiropractic Association
1701 Clarendon Boulevard
Arlington, VA 22209
703-276-8800
www.amerchiro.org

American Massage Therapy Association
820 Davis Street, Suite 100
Evanston, IL 60201-4444
847-864-0123
www.amtamassage.org

American Oriental Bodywork Therapy Association
1010 Haddonfield-Berlin Road, Suite 408
Voorhees, NJ 08043
609-782-1616
www.healthy.net/aobta

American Osteopathic Association
142 E. Ontario Street
Chicago, IL 60611
312-202-8000
www.am-osteo-assn.org

Ayurvedic Institute
11311 Menaul NE, Suite A
Albuquerque, NM 87112
505-291-9698
www.ayurveda.com

British Osteopathic Association
Langham House East
Luton, Bedfordshire
United Kingdom LU1 2NA
1582-488-455

Canadian Osteopathic Association
575 Waterloo Street
London, Ontario N6B 2R2
Canada
519-439-5521

The Center for Mind/Body Medicine
5225 Connecticut Avenue, NW, Suite 414
Washington, DC 20015
202-966-7338
www.healthy.net/cmbm

College of Maharishi Vedic Medicine
Maharishi University of Management
1000 N. Fourth Street
Fairfield, IA 52557
515-472-1150
www.mum.edu

Herb Research Foundation
1007 Pearl Street, Suite 200
Boulder, CO 80302
303-449-2265
www.herbs.org

International Chiropractors' Association
1110 N. Glebe Road, Suite 1000
Arlington, VA 22301
800-423-4690, 703-528-5000
www.chiropractic.org

National Center for Homeopathy
801 North Fairfax Street, Suite 306
Alexandria, VA 22314
703-548-7790
www.homeopathic.org

National Commission for the Certification of
Acupuncturists
11 Canal Center Plaza, Suite 300
Alexandria, VA 22314
703-548-9004
www.nccaom.org

INDEX

ABOUT THE AUTHOR

Jeanne Rattenbury has worked as a magazine writer and an editor since 1989, when she joined the staff of *Chicago* magazine. She started writing about health topics on a freelance basis in 1991. She has reported on unconventional medicine for *Vegetarian Times* magazine and on conventional medicine for *Family Safety and Health* magazine. She is a graduate of Loyola University in Chicago, where she lives with her husband and two daughters.